CISTERCIAN STUDIES SERIES: ONE HUNDRED AND SIX

HARLOTS OF THE DESERT

HARLOTS OF THE DESERT

A study of repentance in early monastic sources

Benedicta Ward S.L.G.

CISTERCIAN PUBLICATIONS INC.

Kalamazoo, Michigan

First published 1987
by A. R. Mowbray & Co., Ltd., Oxford
and Cistercian Publications Inc., Kalamazoo.

Available from the publisher
Cistercian Publications (Distribution)
Saint Joseph's Abbey
Spencer, MA 01562 (USA)

Printed in the United States of America

ISBN 0 87907 606 2

CONTENTS

Preface

The *Lives of the Harlots* are texts about repentance, the return of
everyman to the lost Kingdom. Because of this continuity of theme
with that of the Bible, I have chosen to present here first the account
of Mary Magdalene as the biblical image of the sinful person who
repents. The second text is the account of Mary of Egypt, which is
used as a type of repentance, especially in the liturgy of the Eastern
Orthodox Church. With these I have put three monastic texts on the
same theme of conversion from prostitution to sanctity which circulated as a group among monks in the early Church. I have com-
mented on the texts as part of a general theme of repentance;
translations of the texts are added after each section of commentary.

In each case the stories in the texts I have translated are the end
product of various other forms of the tales, and while I do not intend
to present a critique of the sources, I have included some of the related texts in order to give the longer accounts an authentic setting.
Since it seems to me that there is here a theme central to Christianity, and it is this which I am concerned to analyse rather than the
details of the texts as literature, I have confined my remarks on the
texts, as such, to footnotes. Originally written in Greek, these texts
were translated into Latin and continued to be read through the
Middle Ages, increasing, even, in popularity. I have used the Latin
version of the texts from the *Vitae Patrum* since the focus of this
study is their significance in the West rather than the East: the last
chapter, therefore, is about the texts in the medieval West.

I would like to thank the monks of the Monastery of the Holy
Cross at Chevetogne for their hospitality and assistance while
writing this book, my colleagues and pupils in Oxford for their
patience and encouragement, and my own Community for so
generously giving me continual interest and support, especially
Sister Christine S.L.G., who provided the index.

I first thought of translating these texts after meeting Maria, a
very young girl living in London as a prostitute. One evening she
approached me and asked me to help her get away from a life she

hated. While we talked a car drove up and Maria was taken away by her protectors. I dedicate this book to her, asking that the mercy of God may come upon us all.

Benedicta Ward S.L.G. Oxford, 1987

Abbreviations

Acta SS: Acta Sanctorum Bollandiana, ed. J. Bollandus *et al.*, (61 vols., Antwerp, Brussels etc., 1643– in progress)

BHG: Bibliotheca Hagiographica Graeca (Brussels, 1909)

BHL: Bibliotheca Hagiographica Latina (Brussels, 1901)

Lives: The Lives of the Desert Fathers, translation by Norman Russell, introductory monograph by Benedicta Ward (London, 1980)

PG: Patrologiae cursus completus: series graeca, ed. J. P. Migne (161 vols., Paris, 1857–66)

PL: Patrologiae cursus completus: series latina, ed. J. P. Migne (221 vols., Paris, 1844–6)

Sayings: Sayings of the Desert Fathers, trans. Benedicta Ward (London, 1983)

SC: Sources Chrétiennes (Paris, 1940 ff.)

Wisdom: Wisdom of the Desert Fathers, trans. Benedicta Ward (Oxford, 1986)

World: The World of the Desert Fathers, trans. Columba Stewart (Oxford, 1986)

CHAPTER ONE

The Theme of Repentance

*What is the meaning of this story? These men have none
of our education and yet they stand up and storm the gates
of heaven . . .*[1]

In the autumn of 384 Augustine, a man of thirty, was appointed Professor of Rhetoric in Milan, and to further his career he sent his concubine back to Africa in order to be free to negotiate a respectable marriage. His turbulent spirit continued its search for truth, life, light, but however high his thought ranged, he found that sensual desire held him captive, preventing any real step towards making the dream a reality. Two years later he felt himself still held fast by the bonds of lust:

> My will was perverse and lust had grown from it, and
> when I gave in to lust, habit was formed and when I did
> not resist the habit it became a necessity.[2]

One day this torment was resolved. Augustine was visited by a friend from Africa, Ponticianus, a member of the Emperor's household, who told Augustine a story that amazed him. One afternoon while the Emperor was watching the games in the circus, Ponticianus and three friends went out to stroll in the gardens near the city walls . . .

> As they wandered, the second pair came to a house
> which was the home of some servants of yours, men
> poor in spirit, to whom the kingdom of heaven belongs.
> In the house they found a book containing the life of
> Antony. One of them began to read it and was so fascinated and thrilled by the story that even before he had
> finished reading he conceived the idea of taking upon
> himself the same kind of life and abandoning his career
> in the world.[3]

1

The two who had been converted found their companions
and told them all that had happened. All four were moved and
wept with the impact of freedom that had touched them. The
first two decided at once to follow the way of life of the
monks, and the girls to whom they had been betrothed
caught fire from them and also vowed celibacy. As he
listened, Augustine was struck to the heart. He went away
from his companions, and

> somehow I flung myself down under a fig tree and gave
> way to the tears that were now streaming from my eyes
> ... I stemmed my tears and stood up ... I seized the
> book [St Paul's *Epistles*] and opened it, and in silence I
> read the first passage on which my eyes fell, 'not in revel-
> ling and drunkenness, not in lust and wantonness, not in
> quarrels and rivalries. Rather, arm yourselves with the
> Lord Jesus, and make no provision for the flesh and the
> lusts thereof' (Rom 13. 13, 14). I had no wish to read
> more and no need to do so. For in an instant, as I came to
> the end of the sentence, it was as though the light of con-
> fidence flooded into my heart and all the darkness of
> doubt was dispelled.[4]

Augustine's first action was to tell his close friend, Alypius,
what had happened to him; Alypius also resolved to choose
this ascetic way of life and together they told the news to
Monica, Augustine's mother, who had prayed for that
moment with tears.

This supreme example of dramatic conversion in the life of
the formative theologian of the West was not something
experienced in isolation, as the story itself shows. When
anyone discovers the healing fountains of conversion, it is in
some way through the gift of other people, and the waters of
life thus received overflow in their turn into the lives of
others, to fructify the deserts of human experience; it
becomes a chain reaction, not only for those who hear but for
those who read about the event. At each stage there are tears,
not the tears of self-pity or remorse, but the lifegiving tears
that come from a heart suddenly open to life and love. Ponticianus and his friends wept; so did Augustine; so did Monica.
This account forms part of a literature of events full of tears

and of radiant delight. At each stage this sudden, life-giving, unlooked-for apprehension of God is communicated to others, either by personal contact, or through writing. With the young courtiers the contact was spoken, as was that of Ponticianus to Augustine, and Augustine to Alypius, Monica and their friends: but the communication of life also happened through books; whether the *Life of St Antony*, which the courtiers read and Augustine knew, or by Augustine's own *Confessions*, or by the scriptures which lay behind both. When Augustine wrote the *Confessions* he meant it to be more than an account of his own life; it was a testimony to the power of God and it was public; it was to touch other lives through the ages.

The conversion of Augustine and his friends was profoundly connected with the tradition of conversion in the deserts of Egypt, since its immediate cause was the account of the conversion of Antony of Egypt, the most famous and influential of the desert fathers.

> 'I had heard', Augustine wrote, 'the story of Antony and I remembered how he happened to go into a church while the Gospel was being read and taken it as a counsel addressed to himself when he heard the words, "Go, sell all that belongs to you and give to the poor ... and come and follow me".'[5]

Antony of Egypt, the first christian hermit in Egypt, belongs to a tradition of monastic experience, the essence of which is found in the accounts it produced of repentance and conversion, a turning from an old way of life to a new by the uncovenanted action of God. Accounts of these events were written down and elaborated and passed round among the monks for encouragement. The lives of the harlots which are considered here belong to this ascetic literary tradition, and were used in precisely this way. Like Augustine's account of his own conversion, there are written accounts of the conversion of some of the ascetics of the ancient world which were written down to show the power of the action of God in human lives as an encouragement to others. In order to give a context to the stories·examined in detail here, about the conversion of women who had been prostitutes, it is necessary first to look at the wider context of accounts of monastic conversion in this period.

First, the account given by Athanasius of Alexandria of Antony the Great began with what became the archetypal description of the moment of conversion:

> Antony was an Egyptian by birth. His parents were of good stock and well to do and because they were Christians he himself had been brought up as a Christian. Upon his parents' death he was left alone with a sister who was very young. He was about eighteen or twenty at the time ... One day as he was walking along towards the church, he reflected how the apostles left everything and followed the Saviour and also how the people in Acts sold everything and laid it at the feet of the apostles for distribution among the needy and what great hope is laid up in heaven for such as these. With these thoughts in his mind he entered the church. And it so happened that the Gospel was being read at that very moment and he heard the passage in which the Lord says to the rich man, 'if you will be perfect, go, sell all that you have and give to the poor and come and follow me and you will have treasure in heaven' ... Antony immediately left the church and gave to the townsfolk the property he had from his forebears, keeping only a little of the proceeds for his sister. But once again he entered the church and heard the Lord saying in the Gospel, 'be not solicitous for the morrow'. He could not bear to wait any longer but went out and distributed everything to the poor. Then he devoted all his time to ascetic living near his own house, for there were not yet many monasteries in Egypt and no monk even knew of the faraway desert.[6]

As with Augustine, the turning-point came through the scriptures, the 'sword of the Spirit' (Ephesians 5,6). Moreover, the scriptures were read to Antony by another person, the reader in the church. Antony was not a public sinner nor was he said to be held by the bonds of sexual sin, but he turned from his secure and comfortable life as decisively as Augustine was to do from more explicit sins. His conversion is described as absolute and final; he heard the word of the gospel and obeyed at once, literally and without question.

And his conversion at once became fruitful in the lives of others, whether those of his immediate disciples or those who read the account. A later historian, surveying the effect of the *Life of St Antony*, described it in terms which, by their very hostility, illustrate its force: 'If I may be permitted to use strong language, I should not hesitate to say that no book has had a more stultifying effect on Egypt, Western Asia and Europe than the *Vita S. Antonii*.'[7]

With another of the monks of the desert, the parallel with Augustine, and also with the harlots, is more precise:

> It was said of a certain abba Apollo of Scetis that he had been a shepherd and he was very uncouth. He had seen a pregnant woman, in the field one day and being urged by the devil he had said, 'I should like to see how the child lies in her womb'. So he ripped her up and saw the foetus. Immediately his heart was troubled and, filled with compunction, he went to Scetis and told the fathers what he had done. Now he heard them chanting, 'the years of our age are three score and ten years and even by strength fourscore, yet their span is but toil and trouble' (Ps 90.10). He said to them 'I am forty years old and I have not made one prayer, and now if I live another year I shall not cease to pray to God that He may pardon my sins'. In fact, he did not work with his hands but passed all his time in prayer, saying, 'I as man have sinned; do thou as God forgive'.[8]

This is not the world of the intellectual Augustine nor of the christian Antony, but of the rough peasants of Egypt who formed so large a part of the monastic movement; but there is the same kind of reaction of repentance. There is the hearing of a sentence from the scriptures read aloud by others, there is a final departure from a familiar way of life, there is an entire concentration, from that moment, on the need for mercy. Many of the monks of Egypt began their monastic life out of moments of conversion which are similar, if less extreme. John of Lycopolis, for instance, relates the story of a wild and licentious young man:

> At God's bidding he was struck with compunction for his many sins. He made straight for the cemetery, where he bitterly lamented his former life, throwing himself

down on his face and not daring to make a sound or pro-
nounce the name of God or to entreat him, for he considered himself unworthy even of life itself ... as a
result of this a great number of those who had utterly
despaired of themselves pursued good practices and
lived a virtuous life. They realised in their own lives the
text of Scripture which says, 'whosoever humbleth himself shall be exalted' (cf. Luke 14.11;18.14).[9]

Others about whom we know less in detail present the
same pattern: their conversion, their decision to live only in
order to receive mercy, was for them the beginning of life,
often a life of struggle to make real and actual the fact of that
mercy in their lives. For instance, Moses the Black, who had
been a robber and a murderer, was said to be so tempted to
fornication that he despaired and went to abba Isadore to say
he could not endure it.[10] Amma Sarah turned to the ascetic
life, but spent thirteen years tempted by lust; it was said that
'she never prayed that the warfare should cease but she said,
O God give me strength'.[11]

In each of these accounts of conversion there is a real conviction of need and a correspondingly strong desire for
mercy. So overwhelming is this conviction in the desert that
mercy is the whole life of a monk, that there are stories to illustrate the fate of the monk who is merely 'good'. John of
Lycopolis, for instance, describes a monk who had lived a
very regular and disciplined life in the desert for many years,
but because the essential lesson of total dependence upon him
before whom 'all our righteousness is filthy rags' (Isa. 64.6)
had not been learnt, he fell into sin and into despair. He
allowed a woman who was lost in the desert to enter his cell,
and talked with her and eventually 'he consented inwardly
and tried to unite himself sexually with her'. In the morning,
he despaired of his salvation and returned to the world.[12] In
this story it is a genuinely good monk who falls into sin, but it
is not this which condemns him. Rather, it is the pride which
cannot bear to have fallen and therefore cannot ask for
forgiveness and mercy, that is the failure. As John of Lycopolis remarks, 'One ought not be puffed up by one's own
achievements but always be humble and flee to the furthest
parts of the desert'; not 'if one is tempted by sexual sin' but 'if

one is becoming proud ... We ought not to despair of our salvation...'[13]

Stories were told in the desert of prostitutes who had changed their way of life and turned from degradation to a life of heroic sanctity. In the stories of the harlots this theme of the awareness of the need for mercy is central. Like the good monk described by John of Lycopolis, Maria the niece of Abraham falls because she has simply done good actions without learning this essential lesson, and so she despairs of forgiveness. In the story of Mary of Egypt, the monk Zossima is presented as a good, pious monk, yet lacking the essential experience of an awareness of sin before God, and this he learns only from the example of Mary the harlot, who, by her repentance, has become all that he longs to be and cannot achieve by his own efforts. Where his life had been a continual effort to achieve, she received more by her humble and grateful acceptance of mercy. Thaïs the harlot is seen as entering heaven with glory even while, like Apollo the Shepherd, she is still in her cell praying; 'You who made me, have mercy upon me' (p. 84), and in this it is implied that she is preferred even to Antony the Great.

The stories of the harlots belong to this literature of conversion, and behind them there is, of course, the pattern of the great penitent of the New Testament, Mary Magdalene. Behind her lies the image of the sinful woman who is Israel, unfaithful to the covenant of God. The sinful woman is also Eve, the mother of all the living, and therefore the image is of Everyman, of the human race alienated from the love of God. The accounts of the harlots specifically refer to words, phrases, and incidents in the scriptures to deepen this truth – which does not destroy but deepens their historical validity. Each story was meant to be read or heard by others, so that the moment of grace in these lives might continue to touch others. At the end of the account of Mary of Egypt, for instance, the author says that the monks used to tell the story to visitors 'for their edification' (p. 56) and that he has written it down to benefit those who read it. The stories of extreme sin and extreme repentance were in fact stories of extreme love, and their effect was to be very similar, for those who read them, to the effect of the sight of 'the Prison' upon John

of the Ladder. As a young monk, John visited 'the abode of
the penitents,' 'that is, a special monastery where monks
undertook extreme penances, concentrating only upon repentance; 'he returned very much changed'. 'It seems to me,' he
wrote, 'that those who have fallen and are penitent are more
blessed than those who have never fallen and who do not have
to mourn over themselves, because through having fallen,
they have pulled themselves up by a more sure resurrection.'[14] He recommends consideration of the monks of the
prison who have gone there voluntarily to endure great sufferings in repentance, so that his readers may be encouraged:
'Let us listen, take heed and act – we who may have suffered
an unexpected fall. Rise up and be seated, all you who have
been laid low by your sins. Hear what I have to say, my
brothers. Listen, all you who long to be reconciled with God
again in true conversion.'[15]

The actual sight of penitents or the story told about them
presents the truth about repentance more certainly than an
analysis or theory. Repentance is not a theory to be worked
out but a way of life; that is why the stories about repentance
are more useful than any amount of teaching on the subject.
In them the reader is not instructed directly but shown the
working of God within human lives, with all their subtlety
and variety. It is not a pattern to follow but an experience to
be shared. The people who are within the process of redemption are full of faults, stupidities, sins, and failings; they are
also capable of transfiguration: 'The penitent stands guilty,
but undisgraced'.[16]

NOTES TO CHAPTER ONE

1. Augustine of Hippo, *Confessions*, 8, viii.
2. *ibid.* 8, v.
3. *ibid.* 8. vi.
4. *ibid.* 8, viii.
5. *ibid.* 8, 12.
6. Athanasius, *Life of St Antony*, trans. R. C. Gregg (SPCK, London, 1980).
7. Harnack, quoted by H. Waddell, *The Desert Fathers* (London, 1936) p. 7.

8. *Sayings*, Apollo 2.
9. *Lives*, John of Lycopolis, 37–8.
10. *Sayings*, Moses 1.
11. *ibid.* Sarah 1.
12. *Lives*, 32–6.
13. *ibid.* 36.
14. John Climacus, *The Ladder of Divine Ascent*, trans. Colm Luibheid and Norman Russell (London, 1982), p. 128.
15. *ibid.* pp. 121–2.
16. *ibid.* p. 121.

CHAPTER TWO

St Mary Magdalene; the Biblical Model of Repentance

Beauty consuming itself like incense burned before God in solitude far from the eyes of men became the most stirring image of penance conceivable . . . the generosity of expiation, the gift of tears, were to the Christian a perpetual subject of meditation.[1]

Mary Magdalene has always been one of the most popular of saints, perhaps because of the extremes of her career from prostitute to hermit, from sin to sanctity, from grief to glory. She has been seen from the earliest times, in scripture and in the liturgy, as the one woman who, with the mother of Jesus, shared with the apostles the rare and essential distinction of having been with the Lord. She has been called 'the apostle to the apostles', the 'friend', and even the 'beloved' of Christ, a sinful woman who loved greatly and was forgiven much.

Who was Mary Magdalene? The Middle Ages both contracted her person and expanded her history. Out of the several women called Mary mentioned in the Bible (with the exception of the mother of Jesus) they made one, and then examined the possibilities open to this composite person, elaborating it with enthusiasm and delight. Imagination went so far that a devotee in the 14th century could write:

> I do not trouble myself about chronology in my meditation; it delights me to tell of the Magdalene and what she did at this time according to my fancy... While I think of her I must perforce think of Jesus and His Mother.[2]

Starting from various points in the gospels, Mary Magdalene emerged and lived a life varied by the imagination of the devout. She was celebrated first of all in the liturgy, both at

Easter and on her feast-day, then in sermons and commentaries of the Fathers, from Augustine, Jerome and Gregory to
Anselm and Guibert of Nogent. Her elegant image inspired
prayers such as that of Anselm, passionate lines such as those
of Petrarch. Plays about her meeting with the risen Jesus in
the garden of the resurrection, surely one of the most dramatic moments ever recorded, brought her close to the heart.
At Aix-en-Provence and at Vézelay her relics were venerated
and the glories of architecture added to her renown. Her
name became synonymous with 'prostitute', and houses for
the reformation of fallen women were traditionally under her
patronage. In the 20th century, Kazanzakis has created an
alternative Mary Magdalene; *Godspell* and *Jesus Christ Super-
star* have not ignored her; and Kipling assumes so intimate a
knowledge of her story that he can use the words 'she went
away, supposing him to be the gardener' as the heart-rending
key to a story of the aftermath of the First World War.[3]

What can be learnt about Mary Magdalene in the earliest
documents that mention her, the gospels?[4] The name, Mary
of Magdala, is found in Luke 8.2 and in Mark 16.9. In Luke
she is one of the women who followed Jesus, 'out of whom he
had cast seven devils', and in Mark again she is 'a woman out
of whom he had cast seven devils'; but she is also the one to
whom he first appeared after his resurrection. This gives us a
Mary from Magdala, a woman possessed by seven devils (in
other words, a woman who was cured of the sickness of sin
by Jesus): a forgiven sinner who followed him in his ministry
and met him after he rose from the dead. In the gospel of
John, Mary Magdalene is named in two situations, first with
the mother of Jesus at the foot of the cross, and second in a
more extended account of her meeting with Jesus in the
garden of the resurrection (John 19.25; 20.1–19). So far the
picture is consistent enough: Mary Magadlene cured; a disciple; someone present at the crucifixion; a witness of the resurrection and, according to John, the first to take the news of
the Lord's resurrection to the apostles. Luke also says that she
was among the women who anointed the Lord's body for
burial (Luke 24.10).

Other women mentioned in the bible were conflated with
Mary, and the process by which this accumulation occurred

was at first a grammatical one; they were all linked together by the coincidence of words. For instance, two anonymous women were said to have come to Jesus; the one, early in his ministry (Luke 7.39) to anoint his feet with tears, the other, at the end of the ministry, before the Passion, to anoint his head with ointment (Matthew 26.6–13; Mark 14.3–8). One anointing is said to have taken place in the house of a pharisee, the other in the house of Simon the Leper at Bethany. In the first case the sins of the woman were forgiven 'for she loved much'. She was said, incidentally, to be 'a woman of the city who was a sinner', which is not an obvious phrase meaning prostitute; in fact, she is described by Jesus as having 'many sins', not just one. The second anointing woman is said to have anointed the Lord 'for his burial'. So the idea of forgiveness and great love linked these two with Mary of Magdala; and 'Bethany' connected them all with another Mary, the sister of Martha and Lazarus, those friends of Jesus with whom he stayed in Bethany. The gospel of John tells us that this other Mary had 'anointed the feet of the Lord with ointment and wiped them with her hair' (John 12.13). Although the anointing is here of the feet rather than of the head of Jesus, the anointing women were all seen as Mary of Bethany, the sister of Martha, who was then identified as Mary of Magdala, though on no scriptural authority whatever. This Mary, according to Luke, had also sat at the Lord's feet instead of helping her sister to serve, and he gives Jesus' defence of her, a defence which was to become the classic defence of the contemplative: 'Mary has chosen the better part and it shall not be taken from her' (Luke 10.42), thus linking the forgiven sinful woman with prayer and the heights of contemplation. The word 'anointing' as connected with the feet and head of Jesus suggested also the anointing of the body of Jesus for burial by certain women, among whom all the evangelists number Mary of Magdala (Matthew 28.1; Mark 16.1; Luke 24.10; John 20.1).

It is a curious fact that, although it was always clear in the scriptures that several persons had been combined to make up 'Mary Magdalene', it was quite impossible to think of her as anything other than what myth had made her. This shows a striking instance of the influence of the Fathers of the

Church, both within and outside the liturgy, conditioning the reading of the Bible in such a way that their spiritual interpretations were taken literally. In the Latin tradition, for instance, the homilies of St Gregory the Great in particular emphasized the conflation of Marys for the feast of St Mary Magdalene, but even more so during the readings in the week of Easter:

> Mary Magdalene, a woman of the city which was a sinner, washed out the stain of her sins with her tears by her love of the truth; and the word of truth is fulfilled which says her sins are forgiven for she loved much. She who had previously been cold through sin was afterwards ·aflame with love. For when she came to the sepulchre and found that the Lord's body was not there, she believed that it had been taken away and told the disciples so.[5]

A forgiven sinner, Mary Magdalene anointing the feet of the Lord with tears and becoming the first witness of the resurrection, was presented by St Gregory in a homily concerned with conveying the moral and spiritual application of scripture to a congregation in Rome in the sixth century. The homily was used to provide lessons for the feast of St Mary Magdalene, and the collect for that day firmly identified her with Mary the sister of Martha and Lazarus:

> May we be aided, O Lord we beseech thee, by the intercession of blessed Mary Magdalene in answer to whose prayers thou didst raise her brother Lazarus to life after he had been dead four days.[6]

The same kind of conflation takes place in the sermons of Augustine and the commentaries of Bede, where, as with Gregory, the spiritual and moral application of the text was the main concern and not the historical sense at all. It seems possible to conclude from the commentaries of the Fathers that the early Church saw in this composite Mary a figure of significance beyond her several parts. The central fact of the gospel is that 'Christ Jesus came into the world to save sinners' (1 Timothy 1.15) and here is the most dramatic of all examples of this in action. Here is a woman set free from the

bonds of sin by Jesus, meeting him in a garden as the redeemer of all creation. This figure of a woman who was a
sinner greeted by the new Adam in a garden, is presented as the
perfect balance to that story of grief in a garden in the beginning, when the first man and woman sinned and experienced
death and division. As St Gregory the Great says,

> Lo, the guilt of the human race is cut off whence it pro-
> ceeded. For in paradise a woman gave death to man;
> now from the tomb a woman announces life to men and
> tells the words of the Life-giver just as a woman (Eve)
> told the words of the death-bearing serpent[7]

or, in the more elegant words of Peter Chrysologus, com-
menting on the phrase, 'in the end of the Sabbath, as it began to
dawn towards the first day of the week...' (Matthew 28.1);

> On this later day, a woman runs to grace who earlier ran
> to guilt. In the evening she seeks Christ who in the
> morning knew that she had lost Adam. 'Then cometh
> Mary and the other Mary to the sepulchre' (Matt. 28.1).
> She who had taken perfidy from paradise hastens to take
> faith from the sepulchre; she hastens to snatch life from
> death who had snatched death from life.[8]

Mary Magdalene, for the evangelists and for the Fathers, is
not just a historical character or characters; she is the new
Eve, the first sign of the reversal of the fall of Adam. She is
also, because of her great love, the woman in the Song of
Songs[9], and she is, for the same reason, the Church as well as
the individual soul redeemed from sin.[10]

Why, then, was Mary of Magdala assumed to be a prostitute? In the gospels there is no mention of what kind of devils
had possessed her. Mary of Magdala was said to have had
'seven devils' cast out of her, not just one devil of lust, as is assumed in descriptions of her later; she might have been a murderer, a thief, anything. The phrase, 'a woman of the city'
(*amatole polis*), does not necessarily bear such an interpretation; she is not, after all, described by the more direct word,
hetaira, a prostitute. I suggest that her identification as a prostitute lies deeper, in the imagery of sin throughout the whole
of the scriptures. Mary Magdalene takes to herself the image

of unfaithful Israel, so graphically described by the prophets as a prostitute in relation to God. This image was transferred by the New Testament writers to the whole of humanity in the new covenant, and therefore each soul in sin can be described as a prostitute, as unfaithful to the covenant of love between God and man. It is in this profoundly illuminating sense that Mary of Magdala assumes the character of a prostitute, not because lust is a specially terrible sin but because she is all sinners insofar as all sin is unfaithfulness to the covenant of love. Just as the sin of Eve was described as lust because that image best describes the disobedience of the Fall, so the sins of Mary of Magdala were seen as prostitution; that is, unfaithfulness to the love which is the name of God.

It was, however, a short step from this spiritual under-standing of Mary as a prostitute to a literal view of her career. Moreover, by an unfortunate mistake, she was also thought to have been Mary of Egypt, a later saint whose career re-sembled that of Mary Magdalene too closely for them to remain unconfused. Mary of Egypt, whose life is discussed later (pp. 26–56), was also a sinful woman turned hermit. It was perhaps this link which provided material for the idea of sexual sin as Mary Magdalene's main concern, as distinct from possession by all seven devils. It is also possible that the idea of Mary Magdalene as a prostitute was affected by a tradition found in some fragments, which may come from a gnostic milieux in which Mary Magdalene is referred to as the lover of Christ. In *The Gospel of Philip*, for instance, she is described as Jesus' most intimate companion:

> the companion of the Saviour is Mary Magdalene. Christ loved her more than all his disciples, and used to kiss her often on her mouth.[11]

This text is itself shaped by the imagery of both divine wisdom and the bride of the Song of Songs, but which could also have a more literal interpretation. Although the writings which make such references were not authenticated by common christian belief and liturgical practice in the early Church, and therefore did not affect the medieval tradition in any central fashion, they may reflect a view of Mary Magda-lene equally open to misinterpretation on a popular level.

The Fathers applied the spiritual sense of the scriptures to the composite figure of Mary Magdalene for ends which were not in any way historical; they were rather directed to the meaning of the word of God for the hearer, and historical accuracy quite rightly took second place.[12] But popular imagination had its own way of hearing the subtleties of the Fathers, and in this, as in so many other cases, exercised itself upon the actual history of the person depicted. What the devout of the Middle Ages wanted to know about Mary Magdalene was; who her parents were, her brothers and sisters, where she was born, how brought up and what happened to her after the ascension; all questions which were answered very neatly from a mixture of apocryphal stories, biblical texts, and popular imagination exercised upon the question of what was appropriate, what ought to have happened. It was generally agreed that her parents were called Cyrus and Euchoria, rich and noble people who lived in the castle of Magdala. Mary was the youngest of their three children and she was betrothed to St John the Evangelist; it was in their honour that the wedding feast at Cana was arranged. On that occasion, John left his bride to follow Jesus and Mary, beside herself with resentment, became a prostitute:

> She fled to Jerusalem, where, unmindful of her birth, forgetful of the law of God, she became a common prostitute and of her own free will set up a brothel of sin and made it in truth a temple of demons, for seven devils entered into her and plagued her continually with foul desires.[13]

After some time, Jesus cast out the seven devils from Mary and when he visited Martha and Lazarus for supper, Martha persuaded her erring sister to be present. She came in and, as Honorius of Autun says:

> With bare head and bare feet she came to Him with the precious ointment she had previously brought for use in her wickedness. All things that she had willingly done before in the service of the flesh she now in sorrow turned to the service of the Lord.[14]

So far, the details of the story, however vivid, were at

least loosely connected with the gospels; but for Mary's later career, fancy had full play. What happened to her after the ascension and pentecost? In the Greek tradition Mary was said to have followed the apostle John, her former lover and now her fellow disciple, to Ephesus and to have died there and been buried in the same cave as the Seven Sleepers. Her relics were then said to have been taken from there with those of St John and placed in the church of St Lazarus in Constantinople by the Emperor Leo VI. But the Western tradition was much more lively. In the *Apostolic Life of Blessed Mary Magdalene*[15] written by an anonymous author in the eleventh century, although at first attributed to Rabanus Maurus in the tenth, Mary sailed from Palestine with Martha and Lazarus when persecution of christians began, and came to Marseilles. With them was Maximin, one of the 72 disciples of the Lord. The account says that Lazarus stayed there and was consecrated bishop of that city; Martha pursued a fascinating career in France involving the taming of a dragon; Mary and Maximin, the writer says, continued on their way to Aix where the people made Maximin their bishop. Mary lived a life of prayer and penitence and tears in the caves at Baume and was eventually buried in Aix.[16]

Now, it seems probable that this story was elaborated at the abbey of Vézelay, founded in northern France in 858. The account of it found in the *Translation of St Mary Magdalene* forms the prologue to the story, fabricated by the monks, of the theft of the relics from Aix-en-Provence and their arrival at Vézelay in the mid-eighth century. The writer says that Count Girard of Burgundy, a well-known figure in romance and legend, and abbot Heudo of Vézelay sent the monk Badilus to Aix in the eighth century to see what had become of the relics of this saint during the Saracen attacks. He found the town destroyed and some old men showed him the tomb, deserted and in ruins. On inspection, however, it was found to contain the body of the saint, still incorrupt. That night the saint appeared to him in a dream and asked to be taken to a more seemly place. He therefore took the relics and returned with them to Vézelay.

It is a classic account of *pia furta*, the literary tradition by which a story of secret theft accounts for the supposed translation of relics.[17] All the elements of such a story are there: a secret visit, an abandoned tomb, a dream of a saint directing the theft. In fact, devotion to Mary Magdalene at Vézelay began with the abbot Geoffrey (1037–1052), perhaps out of some personal affection for her. The story of how her relics got to Vézelay was put together in his life-time in order to authenticate the claim of Vézelay to her relics, and to give substance to the cult already drawing pilgrims there. It was eminently successful. In 1050 Leo IX issued a bull on 27 April in which St Mary Magdalene was named as one of the special patrons of Vézelay.[18] Eight years later a bull of pope Stephan recognized the presence of her relics there.[19] The romance of the story told at Vézelay caught popular imagination and brought pilgrims there by the hundreds. The church, one of the glories of gothic architecture, rose quickly, further displaying the glories of the saint. The growth of the temporal domain of Vézelay kept pace with the growth of veneration at the shrine. By 1102, 41 churches and four cemeteries belonged to St Mary Magdalene of Vézelay.[20] In May/June 1107, Paschal II visited Vézelay.[21] In 1131–2, Innocent II was there to consecrate the new pilgrims' church, and in 1146 at Easter, St Bernard of Clairvaux was there for the launching of the second crusade among the flower of Europe – Louis VI with his wife, Eleanor of Aquitaine, and his brother, the Count of Dreux; the bishops of Ostia, Langres and Lisieux; the Counts of Flanders, Toulouse, and Nevers.[22]

But the triumph of Vézelay was not to last. The claim to the saint's relics was challenged and, ironically enough, the challengers made use of just the material Vézelay had invented for its own claims. In 1279 the monks of St Maximin at Aix decided to reclaim their saint from the Burgundian usurpers. Legend asserted the presence for many years of St Mary Magdalene as a hermit in the caves at la sainte Baume and her eventual burial in Aix. All this the monks of Aix and of Vézelay agreed upon; but in Aix they began to say that a new examination of the crypt at St Lazare had revealed the body of a saint giving out the sweet odour of sanctity, which was working miracles and even had beside it a small piece of parchment saying 'Here lies the body of the blessed Mary Magdalene'. They were sorry to have to say it, but the monks of Vézelay were deceived; they had taken a body indeed to Vézelay but it must have been the wrong body.[23] Charles of Salerno, Count of Provence, promoted this new cult centre ardently, and presided over a splendid ceremony when the relics were exposed and venerated.[24] Boniface VIII proclaimed indulgences for the shrine, and Vézelay, the town which had seen the preaching of the second crusade and the launching of the third with its pilgrims and offerings, the town which built one of the most splendid cathedrals of France, took a back seat. It was a matter of finances as well as of prestige between rival monastic institutions, with the intrigues and alliances of church and state on a local, and more than local, level. What is more interesting, from the point of view of the cult of relics, is why the relics were accepted first at Vézelay and then at Aix. They had the same story about their provenance so it was not their historicity that was in debate. It was simply the fact that the bones worked, and were shown to work, miracles. Cures reported at Aix eclipsed the fairly inactive shrine at Vézelay, for new cures are news, and the life-blood of a new shrine lies in its cures.[25]

It is significant that one of the people mentioned in the gospels as forming part of the group of those who had known Jesus, should have been the centre of the rivalry of two monasteries in France. The relics of the apostles were those most prized in the Middle Ages, and Mary Magdalene had been called 'the apostle to the apostles'. To have her patronage, and that included possessing her relics, was a matter of local pride. But Mary Magdalene was not a local saint whose relics might stay forever unchallenged in the place of her burial. Her place in the gospels and in the liturgy, with her feast on 22 July, made her a saint of all Christendom. Her place at the foot of the cross made her a vital part of the focal point of a new style of devotion in the twelfth century. She was a saint for everyman, and her relics were the object of sale, theft and exchange. Fragments of her body were given as marks of high favour to men and institutions all over Europe. One of her arms was exhibited at Fécamp in the twelfth century when St Hugh of Lincoln made an exhibition of himself by gnawing two fragments off it for his own use:

after reverently examining and kissing the much venerated bone he tried unsuccessfully to break it with his
fingers and then bit it first with his molars and then with
his incisors.[26]

The fragments were no doubt then enclosed in the gold reli-
quary ring the bishop had caused to be made for his collection
of relics, which already numbered thirty pieces.[27] In the
twelfth and thirteenth centuries houses for lepers, set up
under the patronage of Lazarus, often had a corresponding
house dedicated to the patronage of his sister for repentant
prostitutes, thus giving the name of a fairly inoffensive town
in Palestine to the penitentiaries and their inmates, the Mag-
dalenes.

Above all, what made Mary Magdalene significant for the
early Church and the Middle Ages was the warm and vivid
image of the beautiful and sinful woman repenting in tears,
and learning the secrets of the heart of God by her silent recep-
tivity before the mystery of love. The weeping penitent
touched the heart, but it was the moment in the garden which
completed the image and turned it into the great wonder of
salvation. It is this moment of theological truth which
formed the centre of the prayer of Anselm of Canterbury to
Mary Magdalene:

> St Mary Magdalene,
> You came with springing tears
> To the spring of mercy, Christ. . .
> How can I find words to tell
> About the burning love with which you sought Him
> Weeping at the sepulchre
> And wept for Him in your seeking? . . .
> For the sweetness of love He shows Himself
> Who would not for the bitterness of tears.[28]

In a meditation of lyrical beauty, Anselm appeals to Mary
Magdalene with all the images that have gathered round her
name from all parts of the scriptures as the patron of all sinners in need of mercy. It is significant that it is not in the
house of Simon that Anselm most readily pictured her forgiveness, but in the garden of the resurrection, where all sins
are forgiven for those 'who love much'.

In this first analysis of the prostitute in christian tradition, it seems that the concern of christians has been with something more fundamental than the sexual sins of a woman mentioned in the Bible in first-century Palestine. Mary Magdalene is a sinner, and takes into herself all the sins of mankind first seen in Eve as that fundamental turning away from God, which the Bible calls adultery. The appeal of Mary is that she sins and finds salvation by the free gift of love; it is not less love but more; and therein is the christian hope.[29]

NOTES TO CHAPTER TWO

1. Emile Mâle, *The Gothic Image*.
2. *The Life of St Mary Magdalene*, translated from an unknown Italian writer of the 14th century by Valentin Hawtrey with an introduction by Vernon Lee (London and New York, 1904), pp. 136–7.
3. Rudyard Kipling, 'The Gardener', in *Debits and Credits* (London, 1987), p. 287.
4. see pp. 22–25 for a summary of relevant texts.
5. Gregory the Great, *Homilies on the Gospels*, Hom. xxv, PL 76, col. 1189.
6. Collect for the Feast of St Mary Magdalene (22 July).
7. Gregory the Great, *Hom.* xxv, PL 76, col. 1194.
8. Peter Chrysologus, *Sermon* lxxiv, PL 52, col. 409.
9. cf. Jerome, *Letter* xxii, PL 22, cols. 410–11 for an interesting use of the image of the bride in the Song of Songs with the figure of Mary of Bethany.
10. Bernard of Clairvaux, *On the Song of Songs*, trans. Kilian Walsh OCSO, vol.1, Sermon 7 (Kalamazoo, 1979), pp. 38ff.
11. From *The Gospel of Philip* c.63, quoted by Elaine Pagels in *The Gnostic Gospels*, Weidenfeld and Nicolson, 1980, p. 84.
12. For the classic discussion of allegorical interpretation of scripture, cf. H. De Lubac, *Exegèse Mediéval* (4 vols. Paris, 1961).
13. Honorius of Autun, *Speculum Ecclesiae: De Sancta Maria Magdalena*, PL 172, col. 979.
14. *ibid.* cols. 980–1.
15. *De Vita Apostolicae Beatae Mariae Magdalenae*, PL 112, cols. 1433–95.
16. The standard work on the cult of St Mary Magdalene is V. Saxer, *Le Culte de Ste. Marie Madeleine en occident des origines a la fin du moyen age* (Auxerre-Paris, 1959), and 'L'Origine des

reliques de Ste. Marie Madeleine à Vézelay dans la tradition historique du moyen âge', in *Revue des Sciences religieuses*, vol. 29 (1955), pp. 1–18, and vol. 32 (1958), pp. 1–39.

17. For recent discussion of the theft of relics (with bibliography), cf. P. Geary, *Furta Sacra* (Princeton, 1976).
18. *Bull of Pope Leo IX*, PL 143, col. 642.
19. *Bull of Pope Stephan*, PL 143, col. 883.
20. For details of the sources for the expansion of the lands of Vézelay, cf. V. Saxer, *Le Culte, op.cit.* pp. 91–2.
21. *ibid.* p. 91.
22. For a description of the launching of the Second Crusade, cf. *Saint Bernard of Clairvaux*, trans. G. Webb and A. Walker (London, 1960), pp. 109–10.
23. V. Saxer, *Le dossier vecelien de Marie Madeleine*, Subsidia Hagiographia 57 (Brussels, 1975), pp. 233–5.
24. *ibid.* pp. 261–2.
25. cf. B. Ward, *Miracles and the Medieval Mind* (Scolar Press, 1980, re-printed 1987).
26. Adam of Eynsham, *Life of St Hugh of Lincoln*, ed. and trans. D. Douie and H. Farmer (Nelson Medieval Classics, 1962, re-printed OUP 1986), pp. 169–70.
27. *ibid.* pp. 168–9.
28. Anselm of Canterbury, *Prayers and Meditations*, trans. B. Ward (London, 1980, reprinted 1986), pp. 201–6.
29. For the evolution of the cult of St. Mary Magdalene, especially in English literature, see H. M. Garth, *St. Mary Magdalene in Medieval Tradition*, John Hopkins University, 1950.

Texts from the gospels relating to the figure of St Mary Magdalene

1 A SINFUL WOMAN:
   a. 'And, behold, a woman in the city, which was a sinner, when she knew that Jesus sat at meat in the Pharisee's house, brought an alabaster box of ointment, and stood at his feet behind him weeping, and began to wash his feet with tears, and did wipe them with the hairs of her head, and kissed his feet, and anointed them with the ointment' (Luke 7.37–38).
   b. '[a certain woman], which had been healed of evil spirits and infirmities, Mary called Magdalene, out of whom went seven devils' (Luke 8.2).

2 ANOINTING WOMEN:

   a. 'Now when Jesus was in Bethany, in the house of Simon the leper, there came unto him a woman having an alabaster box of very precious ointment, and poured it on his head, as he sat at meat' (Matthew 26.6–8).

   b. Luke 7.37ff. [cf. 1a *supra*].

   c. 'And being in Bethany in the house of Simon the leper, as he sat at meat, there came a woman having an alabaster box of ointment of spikenard very precious; and she brake the box, and poured it on his head' (Mark 14.3).

   d. 'Then took Mary a pound of ointment of spikenard, very costly, and anointed the feet of Jesus, and wiped his feet with her hair: and the house was filled with the odour of the ointment' (John 12.3).

3 AT THE CROSS:

   a. 'And many women were there beholding afar off, which followed Jesus from Galilee, ministering unto him: among which was Mary Magdalene (Matthew 27.55,56).

   b. 'There were also women looking on afar off: among whom was Mary Magdalene, and Mary the mother of James the less and Joses, and Salome; (who also, when he was in Galilee, followed him and ministered unto him)' (Mark 15.40,41).

   c. 'Now there stood by the cross of Jesus his mother, and his mother's sister, Mary the wife of Cleophas, and Mary Magdalene' (John 19.25).

4 THE WOMEN AT THE SEPULCHRE:

   a. 'And there was Mary Magdalene, and the other Mary, sitting over against the sepulchre' (Matthew 27.61). 'In the end of the sabbath, as it began to dawn toward the first day of the week, came Mary Magdalene and the other Mary to see the sepulchre' (Matthew 28.1).

   b. 'And when the sabbath was past, Mary Magdalene, and Mary the mother of James, and Salome, had bought sweet spices, that they might come and anoint him' (Mark 16.1).

c. 'Now upon the first day of the week, very early in the morning, they came unto the sepulchre, bringing the spices which they had prepared... It was Mary Magdalene, and Joanna, and Mary the mother of James, and the other women' (Luke 24.1 and 10).

d. 'The first day of the week cometh Mary Magdalene early, when it was yet dark, unto the sepulchre' (John 20.1).

5 AT THE RESURRECTION:

a. 'And the angel answered and said unto the women, [cf. 4a *supra*] Fear not ye: for I know that ye seek Jesus, which was crucified. He is not here: for he is risen, as he said. Come, see the place where the Lord lay. And go quickly, and tell his disciples that he is risen from the dead; and they departed quickly from the sepulchre with fear and great joy; and did run to bring his disciples word' (Matthew 28.5–8).

b. 'And he saith unto them [cf. 3b *supra*] ... Ye seek Jesus of Nazareth which was crucified: he is risen; he is not here: behold the place where they laid him. But go ... tell his disciples and Peter that he goeth before you into Galilee: there shall ye see him' (Mark 16.6–7).

c. 'Why seek ye the living among the dead? He is not here, but is risen ... And they ... returned from the sepulchre and told all these things unto the eleven, and to all the rest [cf. 3c *supra*]' (Luke 24.5,8).

d. 'The first day of the week cometh Mary Magdalene early, when it was yet dark, unto the sepulchre ... two angels ... say unto her, Woman, why weepest thou? She saith unto them. Because they have taken away my Lord and I know not where they have laid him. And when she had thus said, she turned herself back, and saw Jesus standing, and knew not that it was Jesus. Jesus saith unto her, Woman, why weepest thou? Whom seekest thou? She, supposing him to be the gardener, saith unto him, Sir, if thou have borne him hence, tell

me where thou hast laid him, and I will take him away.
Jesus saith unto her, Mary. She turned herself, and saith
unto him, Rabboni' (John 20.1–17).

6 MARY OF BETHANY:

a. cf. 2d *supra*.

b. 'She [Martha] had a sister called Mary, which also sat at
    Jesus' feet, and heard his word' (Luke 10.39; John 11.5).

c. 'Now a certain man was sick, named Lazarus, of
    Bethany, the town of Mary and her sister Martha. (It
    was that Mary which anointed the Lord with ointment,
    and wiped his feet with her hair, whose brother Lazarus
    was sick.) . . . Now Jesus loved Martha, and her sister,
    and Lazarus' (John 11.1,2 and 5).

CHAPTER THREE

St Mary of Egypt;
the Liturgical Icon of Repentance

Thrust back by hands from the sanctuary door
*   Mary of Egypt, that hot whore,*
Fell on the threshold. Priests, candles, acolytes,
Shivered in flame upon her failing sight . . .
*   And when at last she died,*
With burning tender eyes, hair like dark flame,
*   The golden lion came*
And gave that dry burnt corpse to the earth's womb.[1]

During Lent, the great season of penance in the christian
church, the Western liturgy uses the biblical figures of repentance, including Mary Magdalene, to illustrate the theme of
the weeks that lead to Easter; in the East, the fifth Sunday of
Lent also celebrates St Mary of Egypt as the model of repentance. Her life is read on the Thursday of that week at matins
and is presented as an icon in words of the theological truths
about repentance.[2]

Who was this Mary? Her story was told in monastic circles
in the East from the sixth century and circulated very quickly
in the West in its Latin forms. It was so well known as a
model of repentance that some thought it a part of the later
history of Mary Magdalene. Even so educated a man as Honorius of Autun confused the two:

> It is said that after she (Mary Magdalene) with the other
> disciples, saw the Lord ascend into heaven, she received
> the Holy Spirit with the others. Afterwards, out of love
> for Him, she did not wish to see any man, but going into
> the desert she lived for many years in a cave. When a cer-
> tain wandering priest came to her and inquired who she
> was, she answered that she was Mary the Sinner and that
> he had been sent to bury her body. With these words she

departed from this world which she had long despised
entering into glory and with angels singing a hymn she
ascended to the Lord whom she greatly loved.[3]

The eleventh century *Apostolic Life of Blessed Mary Magdalene* indignantly denies such a collation: 'It is very false and
borrowed by creators of fables from the deeds of the Egyptian
penitent'.[4] The main point of the stories is the same: the deep-
est sin is turned by the love of Christ into the greatest glory,
and the story of Mary of Egypt in particular was elaborated to
make this abundantly clear. William of Malmesbury, including a version of the story in his *Miracles of the Virgin Mary* says
'she was wicked simply for the fun of it', a point made clearly
in the liturgical version of the text: 'for nearly seventeen years
... I lived as a fire for public depravity but not at all for
money ... I wanted to do it and I did it for nothing'.[5] Her
repentance was equally dramatic; alone in the desert with a
minimum of food and drink, clad only in her hair, she seemed
to the priest Zossima like an angel or a ghost, glimmering
towards him in the moonlight.

In its most popular Latin version[6], the story of Mary of
Egypt was as follows: in her youth, Mary chose to live a dissolute life in Alexandria until, one day, drawn by curiosity,
she joined some pilgrims going by ship to Jerusalem. On the
way she seduced many of her companions, and continued to
live in this way in Jerusalem. On the day appointed for the
veneration of the Holy Cross[7], Mary went with the others to
the door of the church of the Holy Sepulchre where the relic
of the true cross was to be displayed. She went forward to
enter the church with the other pilgrims, but on the threshold
an invisible force seemed to prevent her from entering. At
once sudden contrition filled her heart and she began to weep,
praying to Mary the Mother of God to help her. Next morning she found she could enter the church and venerate the
cross. At once she left the city and crossed over Jordan, taking
only a little bread which she had bought with some coins a
pilgrim had given her. In the desert she lived for forty seven
years until a priest, Zossima, found her by accident, heard her
story, gave her communion and eventually returned in time
to bury her, a lion helping him to dig her grave.

The story seems to fall into two parts: a sinful woman in the holy sepulchre, and a repentant woman in the desert. There is nothing impossible about the framework of either story, and the two parts of it have parallels elsewhere. Another form of the story containing both parts is to be found in the *Life of St Kyriacus* by Cyril of Scythopolis, written in the mid-sixth century. It is less detailed than the version of Sophronius, but follows the same lines. It was told in a monastic milieux:

> I think it good to mention here an edifying tale which abba John told me. When we were walking in the desert, he showed me a certain place which he told me was the tomb of blessed Mary. Full of astonishment, I then asked him to tell me about her. Here is what he said in reply: 'A little while ago, when I was going with my disciple Pananmon to the house of Kyriakos, looking into the distance we saw a human being near a wild tamarisk tree. We thought it was one of the anchorites of the desert – there were many thereabouts – and we hastened then to go and greet him. But when we approached the place, he disappeared. Seized with fear and terror, we gave ourselves up to prayer; we supposed we had had contact with an evil spirit. When we had said "amen" we looked around on all sides and we discovered an underground cave and we guessed that this true servant of God had thrust himself in there to hide from us. We approached the cave and called to him, and at the same time urged him in these words: "Do not deprive us of your blessing, father, and of the benefit of talking with you." At last he answered us: "What do you want of me? I am a woman." Then she asked us, "Where are you going?" and we replied, "To the cell of Kyriakos, but, first tell us your name and how you live and how you came here." "Go away," she said, "and when you return, I will tell you all that." But when we protested that we certainly would not go away without learning her story, she replied, "I am called Maria; I used to be a canoness of (the church of) the holy Resurrection of Christ, and by the fault of the devil I became an object of scandal to many. Fearing that, although I had already done penance for the cause of the scandal, I would add sin to sin (Eccl. 3,29) I prayed to God that He would

remove the cause of the scandal. Then one day when my
heart was full of compunction and the fear of God, I
went down to holy Siloam, filled a jar with water there,
and I also took a basket of small loaves and confiding
myself to God I left the holy city by night. It was He
who led me here and lo, I have been here 18 years and by
the grace of God the water does not fail me nor are the
loaves diminished in the basket until this day. I have seen
no other being until yourselves today. Now go," she
said, "and accomplish your errand and on your return,
come and see me." At her words, we went on to the cell
of abba Kyriakos, and among other things we also told
him this story. Abba Kyriakos marvelled and said,
"Glory to thee, my God, who dost keep hidden such
great sanctity. But go, my children, and do as she told
you." We received the blessing of the old man and went
back to the cave. We knocked, as is the custom at the
cells of the anchorites. Receiving no reply, we crept
inside and we found that the woman was dead. As we
did not know how to lay her out and bury her, we went
on to our lavra of Souka and told them all that had happened. We went back with the funeral trappings and
interred her in her cave, filling up the door with stones.'

Lo, that is what abba John told me, and as I have said, I
thought it necessary to put it into writing to move to
compunction the hearers and the recorder and to give
glory to Christ who gives patience to the end to those
who love Him.[8]

This story of the sinner from the Holy Sepulchre who lives
out her repentance secretly in the desert is further elaborated
in a later version. The story of a nun seduced in Jerusalem was
apparently current among the desert fathers and this version
elaborates the main ideas in many details.

An anchorite told this story to the brothers: 'When I was
living in the desert on the slopes of Arnona, one day a
weakness of soul came upon me and my thoughts said to
me, 'Go for a walk in the desert'. I came to a dried up
stream; it was an advanced hour in the evening and by
the light of the moon I fixed my eyes on a distant object
and I saw that it was sitting on a rock. Then I reflected
that even if it was indeed a lion, I ought not to be afraid
but to entrust myself to the grace of Christ. So I

approached the rock, and by the side of it there was a narrow opening. At once the being I had seen afar off hid itself in this cave. When I reached the top of the rock, I found there a basket full of bread and a jar of water which showed me that it must be a human being. I called to him, 'servant of God, be so kind as to come out so that I may be blessed by you'. He was silent but when I had renewed my appeal several times, he answered me thus: 'Excuse me, father, but I cannot come out'. When I asked why, he said, 'You must know that I am a woman and that I am naked'. At these words I rolled up the cloak I was carrying, and threw it into the opening in the rock, saying to her, 'here, cover yourself and come out' and she did so. When she had come out, we offered a prayer to God and we sat down. Then I asked her, 'My mother, of your kindess, tell me what has happened to you. How long have you been here? Why did you undertake this journey? And how did you find this cave?' She began to tell me about herself thus: 'Once I was a consecrated virgin living in the Holy Sepulchre. One of the monks who had his cell at the gate got to know me. I used to meet him so often that it reached the point where we fell into sin. I would go to his house and he would come to mine. One day as I was going to his cell as usual I heard him weeping before God and making his confession to Him. I knocked on the door, but he, because of what he had done with me, did not open it to me at all. He went on weeping and confessing. Seeing this, I said to myself, 'He is repenting of his sins but I do not repent of mine. He is lamenting his faults; shall I not also afflict myself?' Re-entering my cell alone, I dressed myself poorly and filled this basket with loaves and this jar with water, and then I went into the Holy Sepulchre. There I prayed, asking that the great God, the wonderful, who came to save those who were lost and to raise up those that are fallen, He who hears all those who address themselves to Him in truth, that He would show mercy towards me, a sinful woman, and if He should find the repentance and transformation of my soul acceptable, that He would bless these loaves and this water so that they would last me to the end of my life, so that no necessity of the flesh or needs of hunger should give me a pretext for inter-rupting perpetual praise. After that I went into Holy

Golgotha where I offered the same prayer and touching the top of the Holy Stone, there I invoked the holy Name of God. Then having reached Jericho and crossed over Jordan, I journeyed the length of the Dead Sea, for at that time the water was not very high. I crossed the mountains and wandered in the desert and I had the good fortune to find this dried up stream. When I climbed this rock, I found this cave here and when I went into it its narrowness pleased me greatly, for it made me think that the good God had offered it to me as a place of refuge. I have been here thirty years without having seen anyone except yourself at this hour. The basket of loaves and the jar of water have sufficed for my needs until now without failing me. After a time my clothes wore out but my hair had grown and I was covered with it in such a way that neither heat nor cold made me suffer by the grace of Christ.'

After these words she invited me to take some of the loaves, for she sensed that I was very hungry. We ate and drank equally. Once, I looked into the basket and saw that the loaves remained as they had been and also the water had not diminished and I praised God. I wanted to leave her my old robe but she would not have it. She said, 'You will bring me new clothing', which pleased me very much and I begged her to wait for me just there. We offered a prayer to God and I went away, marking all the way my path for my return. I went back to the church of the near by village and told the priest about the matter. He told the faithful that certain of the saints were living naked and that those who had too many clothes should offer them to them. The friends of Christ gave many clothes diligently and I took what was necessary and went off joyously in the hope of seeing again this spiritual mother. But I could not find the cave again although I wore myself out seeking it. And when at last by chance I saw it, the woman inspired by God was no longer to be found there; her absence affected me deeply. Some days later some anchorites came to visit me, and they told this story: 'When we came to the edge of the sea, we saw by night in the desert an anchorite whose hair covered him; when we begged him to bless us, he fled quickly, entering a little cave which we found near by. We wanted to go in but he implored us, saying, 'Oh

servants of Christ, do not disturb me! Lo, on top of the
rock is a basket of loaves and a jar of water; please be
good enough to serve yourselves.' He offered a prayer
for us to God, and when we reached the top we found
things as he had said. We sat down and although we ate,
the bread did not diminish, and although we drank of
the water in the jar it remained the same. For the rest of
the night we were silent. At dawn we got up to be
blessed by the anchorite and we found him asleep in the
Lord. Also, we discovered that he was a woman who
had been naked and who had covered herself with her
hair. We received a blessing from her body and rolled a
stone to the entry, to the cave. Then, having offered a
prayer to God, we came away.

Then I understood that he spoke of the holy mother,
the former consecrated virgin, and I told them what I
had learned from her. Together we glorified God to
whom be glory to ages of ages. Amen.'[9]

Such stories contain elements which are combined in the
long account of Mary of Egypt by Sophronius, which
became the text used in the liturgy for Lent. Behind the literary form there are various historical details, among them the
fact that Alexandria and Jerusalem, like most great cities, con-
tained women who were prostitutes[10]; and the fact that the
impact of Christianity on Egypt and Palestine very often took
the form of flight to the desert.[11] The moment of conversion,
as well as the details of life before and after that moment, are
heightened in the narrative to emphasise the need for redemption in everyman and the power of the redeeming mercy of
Christ for all, but there is no need therefore to deny a certain
historicity to the stories.[12]

The story of Mary of Egypt lends itself to even more dramatic and vivid presentation than the accounts of the virgin
of Jerusalem. It first presents the independent Egyptian girl,
walking through the city with her spindle by which she
earned her living, always ready for the next sexual adventure,
teasing the sailors to take her on board ship for Jerusalem for
yet more. In Jerusalem, among the crowds at the feast, the
story describes Mary as shocked by the impact of reality,
turning at once towards the desert to struggle alone with the

lust and luxury within herself, among the rocks and sands. The meeting with Zossima is no less vivid: Mary, alive and awake to life, is courteous when she meets the good, controlled, pious monk from a conventional monastic setting; she talks with him by moonlight, telling her story for the first time, always careful not to shock him; and Zossima, dazed with love and adoration, returns at her bidding, as docile and humble as a lover.

But the story of Mary of Egypt is of deeper significance than simply a dramatic tale of a lust turned into love. It is clearly packed with intricate symbols, the most important of which is the contrast of the good, self-satisfied monk who relies for salvation on his own works, with Mary the sinful woman who receives the simple gift of salvation from Christ without any acts, self-exploration, sacraments or prayers, but only because of her great need. Other symbols underline this central theme: Mary takes with her into the desert three loaves of bread which, like the loaves of the prophet Elijah, do not diminish; she passes over the waters of Jordan, the symbol of baptism; she is seen walking on the waters, and at peace with all creation; and it is a lion that comes out of the desert for her burial, the sign of the prince of peace. These details of christian significance would not be lost upon the audiences who heard the story.

This story belongs to the monastic tradition insofar as the monk is the one among christians who sees himself as most in need of mercy, as the penitent, as the sinner, and as the one, therefore, who has only mercy to give. Even the blinding and cramping habit of lust, this story says, can be broken, and the person set free for love and for life. The only necessity is real awareness of need and therefore the possibility of receiving the salvation of Christ. Among the monks there were those who found the story fitted their actual experience very closely: Sarah, Moses and Apollo, for instance, who had each, in one way or another, sinned in a public and dramatic way. Moreover they saw the image of the prostitute as a way of describing inner experience:

> There was in the city a courtesan who had many lovers.
> One of the governors approached her saying, promise

me you will be good and I will marry you. She promised this and he took her and brought her to his home. Her lovers, seeing her again, said to one another, let us go to the back of the house and whistle for her. But the woman stopped her ears and withdrew to the inner chamber and shut the door. The old man said that this courtesan is our soul, that her lovers are the passions, that the lord is Christ, that the inner chamber is the eternal dwelling place, those who whistle are evil demons but the soul always takes refuge in the Lord.[13]

The story of Mary of Egypt combines elements found in various sources, behind which there are real and historical women who were both prostitutes and penitents; the story has been enlarged and given details which increase the significance of the theme of repentance with reference to the edification of the reader or hearer. Like the history of St Mary Magdalene, it conveys theological truth about salvation with a human face, and one which is above all relevant to those who listen:

The power of Thy Cross, O Christ, has worked wonders, for even the woman who was once a harlot chose to follow the ascetic way. Casting aside her weakness, bravely she opposed the devil; and having gained the prize of victory, she intercedes for our souls.[14]

NOTES TO CHAPTER THREE

The Greek text of the *Life of St Mary of Egypt* is printed in PG 87 (3), cols. 3693–3726.

The Latin text of the *Life of St Mary of Egypt*, translated by Paul the Deacon from the Greek of Sophronius, is printed in PL 73, cols. 671–90. (*BHL* 545).

There is an English translation from Slavonic in *St Andrew of Crete (the Great Canon), St Mary of Egypt (the Life)*, by Sr Katherine and Sr Thekla, with a valuable commentary (The Greek Orthodox Monastery of the Assumption, Filgrave, Newport Pagnell, Bucks., 1974).

There is a translation into French by A. d'Andilly, in *Les Vies des Saints Pères des Deserts et quelques Saints, écrits par des Pères de l'Eglise* (1644), re-edited by J. Lacarrière, 1983.

There is a valuable linguistic study of the different versions of the *Life* through the Middle Ages, P. F. Dembrowski, *La Vie de Ste. Marie Egyptienne* (Droz, 1977).
(Two romances round the story of Mary of Egypt are: A. Chedid, *Les Marches de Sable* (Flammaroin, 1981), and J. Lacarrière, *Marie d'Egypte* (Lattes, 1983).

1. John Heath-Stubbs, 'Maria Aegyptica' in *The Swarming of the Bees* (London, 1950), p. 15.
2. Canon of St Mary of Egypt, in *The Lenten Triodion*, trans. Mother Mary and Bishop Kallistos Ware (London, 1979), pp. 447–63.
3. Honorius of Autun, 'De Sancta Maria Magdalena', in *Speculum Ecclesiae*, PL 172, col. 979.
4. *De Vita Apostolica B. Mariae Magdalenae*, PL 122, col. 1433.
5. William of Malmesbury, 'Miracles of the Blessed Virgin Mary', text and translation by P. Carter, unpublished thesis (Oxford, 1970), vol. 1, no. 40, 'Mary of Egypt'.
6. *Vita S. Mariae Aegyptiacae, Meretricis*, PL 73(1), cols. 671–90.
7. This may be the feast of the Exaltation of the Holy Cross celebrated on 14 September since the seventeenth century.
8. Cyril of Scythopolis, *Vie de Kyriakos*, trans. A. J. Festugière (Paris, 1963), xviii–xix, pp. 50–1.
9. BHG 1449, x. (I owe this transcription to the kindness of a friend).
10. cf. Sarah Pomeroy, *Goddesses, Whores, Wives and Slaves* (with bibliography), (London 1973).
11. For conversion in Egypt cf. *Lives of the Desert Fathers*, preface by B. Ward (London, 1981).
12. For the difference between hagiography and biography, see B. Ward, *Miracles and the Medieval Mind* (London, 1980, reprinted 1987), pp. 166–92.
13. *Sayings*, John the Dwarf, 16.
14. Canon of St Mary of Egypt, *Lenten Triodion*, p. 448.

English translation of the *Life of St Mary of Egypt* by Sophronius, bishop of Jerusalem, translated into Latin by Paul, deacon of the holy church of Naples.

It is good to keep close the secret of a king, but to reveal gloriously the works of God (Tobit 2). This is what the angel said to Tobit after his eyes had been miraculously healed from blindness after the dangers through which he had led him and from which he had delivered him because of his piety. Not to keep the secret of a king is a dangerous and fearful matter. But to keep silent about the miraculous works of God, that is dangerous to the soul. This is why, moved by dread of keeping silent about the things of God, and remembering the punishment promised to the servant who took a talent from the lord and buried it, fruitlessly hiding what had been given him to work with, I will not be silent about the holy tale which has reached us. No one should have any doubts about believing me, for I am writing about what I have heard, and no one should think in astonishment over the magnitude of the miracles that I am inventing fables. God deliver me from inventing or falsifying an account in which his name comes! But it seems to me unreasonable to think basely and unworthily about the majesty of the Incarnate Word of God, and not to believe in what is told here. If, however, such readers of this narrative are found, who are so overcome by the miraculous nature of this account that they will not want to believe it, may the Lord be merciful to them! For they consider the infirmity of human nature and think that miracles related about people are impossible. But now I shall start on my tale of events which took place in our own time, as they were revealed to me by good men experienced from childhood in godly words and deeds. They must not try to justify their lack of faith on the grounds that miracles cannot happen in our own generation. For the grace of the Father, flowing from generation to generation through holy souls, makes friends of God and prophets, as Solomon teaches (Wisd. 7.27). But now it is time to begin on this holy tale . . .

Cap. I. Among those who lived as monks in Palestine, there was an old man renowned for his way of life and gift of words; from his infancy he was nourished in the monastic way of life and its works. (He was called Zossima but, in spite of his name, no one should think that I am referring to that Zossima who was at one time guilty of doctrinal error; that was one Zossima, this was another Zossima, and they had nothing in common except the same name.) This Zossima lived in one of the monasteries of Palestine from the begin-

ning of his conversion, and having passed through the whole
of monastic discipline, he became established in every kind of
abstinence. From childhood he observed in everything the
rule handed on canonically, carrying out without blame the
contest of perfect monastic discipline. And he added much
from his own experience, seeking to subdue the flesh to the
spirit. Nor was he known to have offended in any way. So
perfect was he in all monastic behaviour, that many monks
from monasteries of the aforementioned region and even
from distant parts often came to him, drawn by his example
and his teaching, to put themselves under the direction of his
greater discipline.

Cap. II. While he occupied himself with all this, he never
ceased from meditation on the sacred words, whether he was
lying down or getting up or holding his work in his hands. If
however you want to know on what kind of food he fed,
know that he had only one occupation, unflagging and
unceasing, always praising God and meditating on the divine
word. Often, they say, the old man was found worthy of
divine visions, illuminated from on high for, according to the
word of the Lord, 'Blessed are the pure in heart, for they shall
see God' (Matt. 5.8). How much more is this true of those
who keep their bodies cleansed and ever sober; they will see
with the unsleeping eye of the soul visions from on high,
having in them the pledge of the bliss that awaits them. Zossima used to tell how when he was hardly weaned he was
placed in that monastery, where he lived until his fifty-third
year, following an ascetic way of life. It was then that he
began to be tormented by the thought that it seemed as if he
had attained perfection in everything and needed no teaching
from anyone. And so, as he himself said, he began to say to
himself: 'Is there a monk on earth capable of affording me
benefit or passing on to me anything new, some kind of spiritual achievement of which I either do not know or in which I
have not succeeded as a monk? Surely there can be found
among the men of the desert one surpassing me in his deeds?'
While he was turning over this and similar thoughts, someone stood before him and said, 'Zossima, you have done as
well as any man can, you have done well in the whole of the
monastic way. But among human beings, no-one can attain

perfection. A greater ordeal lies ahead of you, although you
do not know this. And so that you may know how many and
varied are the ways to salvation, leave your native land, go
out of your father's house, like Abraham, glorious among the
patriarchs, and go to the monastery which lies near the river
Jordan'.

Cap. III. As soon as he had ceased speaking, Zossima left
the monastery where he had lived since childhood and having
reached Jordan, the holy river, he set out to him who had
called him, along the road to the monastery to which he had
been ordered to go. He knocked on the door of the monastery
and saw first the door-keeper, who took him to the abbot.
The abbot received him, and took note of his appearance and
behaviour, for he made the customary prostration, bowing
down according to the monastic rule, and begged him to pray
for him. Then the abbot asked him 'Where have you come
from, brother, and for what purpose have you come to our
humble monastery?' Zossima answered, 'There is no need to
say where I have come from, but I have come in order to
make spiritual progress. For I have heard concerning you
things worthy of glory and honour, which could draw a soul
to intimate familiarity with Christ our God.' The abbot said
to him, 'God alone who heals human infirmity will reveal,
brother, His divine will to you and to us and teach us how to
do what is right. Man cannot help man unless, soberly and
constantly, each brings his attention to bear on what is right
and proper and has God as his fellow-worker in his labour.
But if, as you say, it was the love of God that moved you to
visit us humble old monks, stay with us and the Good Shepherd will feed us all by the grace of his Spirit, he who laid
down his life to save us and who knows his sheep by name.'
When the abbot had said this, Zossima again prostrated,
asked his prayers, said 'amen' and went to live in the monastery.

Cap. IV. There he saw old men, glorious in the life of
action and also of contemplation, fervent in spirit, serving the
Lord. They sang psalms without ceasing, standing all night
and they always had some work in their hands and unceasing
prayer in their mouths. There was no idle word there, no
thought of gold or silver, in that house there was no concern

about business. The expenses of the whole year, the profits, or any worry about temporal life was unknown to them even by name. For all of them there was only one aim to which all were hastening: to be in the body as a corpse, to die completely to the world and everything in the world. They were not without the food that fails not, the Word of God; they fed their bodies only with bread and water; for each one burned with the love of God.

Cap V. On seeing this, according to his own words, Zossima was very edified, and strove to advance, hastening in his own race, for he had found companions who were the best of all workers in paradise. Some days passed, and the time approached when it is the custom for Christians to keep the holy fast, preparing themselves for the day of the divine Passion and saving Resurrection. The gates of the monastery were always kept closed to allow the monks to work in peace; they were only opened when a matter of real necessity forced a monk to go outside the monastery. The place was a desert and not only out of reach from most of the neighbouring monasteries but even unknown. The monks had a rule and I think it was because of this that God had led Zossima there.

Cap VI. What the rule was and how it was kept I shall now tell you. On the Sunday which gave its name to the first week of Lent, the Divine Mysteries were celebrated in church as usual and everyone received the most pure and life-giving mysteries. And it was also the custom to eat a little food. After this they all met in church and having prayed fervently with prostrations, the old men kissed each other and the abbot, embracing each other and bowing deeply, and each one asked the others to pray for him, and to support him, as they shared the coming conflict. Then last of all the monastery gates were opened and singing in harmony the psalm, 'the Lord is my light and my salvation, whom shall I fear? The Lord is the strength of my life, of whom then shall I be afraid?' and so on, they all went out of the monastery. They left one or two brothers in the monastery, not to guard their property (there was nothing there to attract thieves) but so as not to leave the church without services. Each one took with him whatever food he could and wanted. One carried a little bread for his bodily needs, another figs, another dates, and another grain steeped in water. The last one at the end had nothing but his own body and its tattered clothing and when his nature demanded food, he fed on whatever grew in the desert. But for them all there was one rule and command inflexibly observed by all: not to know about each other, or how the others lived and fasted. At once they crossed the Jordan and then parted from each other over the wide expanse of the desert and not one approached another. If one did notice a brother afar off coming towards him, then he turned aside; each lived by himself and with God, singing psalms all the time and hardly touching food. After they had passed all the days of the fast like this, they returned to the monastery the Sunday before the life-giving Resurrection of the Saviour from the dead, when the church has ordained that the feast with palms should be celebrated before the Feast. Each returned with the fruits of his own conscience, knowing how he had laboured and by which labours he had sown seed in the ground. No one asked anyone else how he had succeeded in the trial he had set himself beforehand.

Cap. VII. This was the rule of the monastery and it was very strictly observed. Each of them fought in the desert against himself before the judge of the fight, God; and he did not seek to please other people by fasting in front of them. For whatever is done for the sake of other people, to please human beings, is not only of no benefit but can lead to severe punishment. So Zossima, also, according to the rule of the monastery, crossed the Jordan, taking a little food with him for the journey for the needs of the body, and the poor clothes he was wearing. He kept the rule, walking through the desert and allowing only the time for food that nature demanded. He slept at night lying on the ground and sleeping for a short time, wherever he happened to be in the evening. In the morning he set out again on his way burning with the desire that did not grow less, to go further. As he himself said, something in his soul urged him to go deep into the desert. He hoped he might find some father there who would fulfil his longing. So he went on tirelessly, as if he were hurrying towards a well-known inn. He had already walked for twenty days when he stopped at the sixth hour and turned towards the east for the customary prayers. He always interrupted his journey at the customary hours of the day and rested a little from his labours, standing, singing psalms or praying upon his knees. And as he sang, without turning his eyes from heaven, he saw on the right from where he stood the shadow of a human body. At first he was troubled, thinking that he saw the appearance of a devil and he trembled. But he protected himself with the sign of the Cross, and chased away fear (his prayers were now over) and he saw that there really was some kind of being walking along at mid-day. It was a woman and she was naked, her body black as if scorched by the fierce heat of the sun, the hair on her head was white as wool and short, coming down only to the neck.

Cap. VIII. On seeing this apparition, Zossima began to run swiftly in the direction in which what he had seen that it was going, and he rejoiced with unspeakable joy. Throughout those days he had not seen a human face once, nor an animal, nor a bird, not even the shadow of a creature. He longed to know who it was that had appeared to him hoping that some great mystery would be revealed to him. But when the apparition saw Zossima approaching, it began to run quickly into the depth of the desert. Zossima forgetting his age, and not thinking of the difficulties of the route, ran very fast, in order to catch up with the fugitive. As soon as he drew near, it ran away. Zossima ran faster and soon he drew near to the one that fled. When Zossima had run near enough for his voice to be heard, he began to shout, in tears, 'Why are you running away from an old man, a sinner? Wait for me, servant of God, whoever you are, in the name of God for whose sake you live in the desert. Wait for me, infirm and unworthy as I am, I beg you, in the name of your hope of reward for your labour. Stop and grant me, an old man, a prayer and blessing for the sake of God who despises no-one.' So Zossima begged with tears and they both ran on to a place that looked like the bed of a dried up stream. (Where could a stream have come from in that land? The ground there had that appearance naturally.) When they reached that place, the fugitive went down and up the other side of the ravine and Zossima, exhausted and unable to run further, stopped on this side, adding tears to tears and increased his sighs with

such sighs that his grief might be heard much more since the
sound was now nearby.

Cap. IX. Then the fugitive spoke: 'Father Zossima, forgive
me, for God's sake, but I cannot turn round and show myself
to you, for I am a woman and, as you see, with the shame of
my body uncovered. If you wish to answer the prayer of a
sinful woman throw me the cloak you are wearing so that I
can cover my woman's weakness and turn and have your
blessing.' At this dread and anxiety fell on Zossima, as he said
himself, when he heard her calling him by his name of Zossima. But he was a man of good intelligence and wise in the
ways of God, so he decided that she would not have called
him by his name, when she had never either seen him or heard
of him before, unless she was enlightened by the grace of
insight. He obeyed her request at once, and took off the old
and tattered cloak he was wearing and threw it to her, turning
his back. She took it and partially hid the nakedness of her
body with it and then turned to Zossima and said, 'Why do
you want to see a sinful woman, father? What do you want to
learn from me or see, that you were not afraid to undertake
such a heavy task?' He knelt down and asked her to give him
the customary blessing. She also knelt down. So they both
remained on the ground asking one another for a blessing.

Cap. X. After a long time the woman said to Zossima,
'Father Zossima, it is proper for you to give the blessing and
say the prayer, for you have the dignity of the office of a
priest, and for many years you have stood at the holy table
and offered the sacrifice of Christ.' These words threw Zossima into greater dread, he trembled and was covered with a
sweat of death. But at last, breathing with difficulty, he said
to her, 'O Mother in the spirit, it is plain from this insight
that all your life you have dwelt with God and have nearly
died to the world. It is plain above all that grace is given you
since you called me by my name and recognised me as a priest
although you have never seen me before. But since grace is
recognised not by office but by gifts of the Spirit, bless me,
for God's sake, and pray for me out of the kindness of your
heart.' So the woman gave way to the wish of the old man,
and said, 'Blessed is God who cares for the salvation of souls'.
Zossima answered 'Amen', and they both rose from their

knees. The woman said to the old man, 'Why have you come to see me, a sinner, sir? Perhaps it was the grace of the Holy Spirit which brought you to perform a certain service for me in due time? Tell me, how are the most Christian tribunes and emperors ruling now? How does the church care for its flock?' Zossima said to her. 'By your holy prayers, mother, Christ has given lasting peace everywhere. But hear the request of an unworthy monk and pray to the Lord for the whole world and for me, a sinner, that my wandering through the desert should not be without fruit.' She answered him, 'It is only right, Father Zossima, that you who have the office of a priest should pray for me and for all; but we must be obedient so I shall willingly do what you bid me.' With these words, she turned to the East and raising her eyes to heaven and stretching up her hands she began to pray moving her lips in silence, so that almost nothing intelligible could be heard. So Zossima could not understand anything of her prayer. As he said, he stood there trembling, looking at the ground and saying nothing. He also swore, calling on God as a witness, that when she seemed to him to be continuing steadfastly in prayer, he raised his eyes a little from the ground and saw that she had risen a cubit from the ground and was standing praying in the air. When he saw this, even greater dread seized him and he fell to the ground, covered with sweat and terrified, not daring to say anything, but saying within himself, 'Lord, have mercy!'

Cap. XI. As he lay on the ground, the old man was troubled by the thought that this might be an evil spirit and the prayer an illusion. But the woman turned round and helped the monk up and said, 'Why are your thoughts troubling you, father, and deceiving you about me, that I may be an evil spirit and my prayer false? Be assured, sir, that I am just a woman and a sinner, but protected by holy baptism. I am not a spirit but earth and ashes, entirely flesh, in no way calling to mind a spirit of phantasy.' With these words, she made the sign of the cross on her brow and eyes, lips and breast, saying, 'God deliver us, Father Zossima, from the evil one and his emissaries, for his envy of us is great.' When he heard and saw this, the old man fell on the ground and embraced her feet with tears, saying, 'I beg you, in the name

of the Lord Jesus Christ, who is indeed our Lord, born of a
Virgin, for whose sake you clothed yourself in this nakedness, for whose sake you have wasted your flesh in this way,
do not hide who you are from your servant or where you
came from, when and how you came to this desert; tell me
everything, so that the wonderful works of God may be
manifest, for as it is written, if wisdom is kept hidden and
treasure a secret, what profit is there in them?' (Ecclesiasticus
20.10) I beg you to tell me everything, for God's sake. For
you will not be telling me out of vainglory or for praise but to
satisfy me, a sinner and unworthy. I believe that God, for
whom you live and whom you serve, has brought me into the
desert for the purpose of revealing to me the things He has
done for you . . . It is not in our power to oppose God's pro-
vidence. If it were not pleasing to the Lord Christ to reveal
you and what you have achieved. He would not have allowed
anyone to see you and He would not have given me the
strength to accomplish such a journey, I who never wished
nor dared to leave my cell.'

Cap. XII. When he had said this and more, the woman
raised him up and said, 'I am ashamed, my father, to tell you
about the infamy of my deeds. But as you have already seen
my naked body, I shall also lay bare before you my deeds, so
that you may know with what shame and contrition my soul
is filled. It is not because of vainglory, as you have realised,
that I want to tell you about myself, for what have I got to be
vainglorious about, having been chosen as a vessel of the
devil? I know, too, that when I begin my story you will run
away from me, as a man runs from a snake; your ears will not
bear to hear the wickedness of my deeds. I tell you, I shall not
keep quiet about anything, begging you first of all to pray for
me without ceasing, that mercy may be found for me on the
day of judgement.' The old man wept without restraint.
Then the woman began to tell him what had happened to her,
thus:

Cap. XIII. 'My homeland, father, was Egypt. I lived with
my parents but when I was only twelve years old I spurned
their care and went into Alexandria. I am ashamed to think
how I first lost my virginity there and how I was on fire with
untiring and clamorous desire for lust, for it cannot be told

briefly. Let me only say this, so that you may understand the insatiable fire within me: for more than seventeen years, I passed my life openly tarrying in the fires of lust. I had not lost my virginity for any gift of money, for I frequently refused what they wanted to give me. I did this with as many as I could get to come to me. Do not think that I was at all rich, for I lived by begging or sometimes by spinning threads of flax. It was just that what I did, I did out of insatiable desire. I wanted to wallow in this trough and that to me was life. I thought any kind of desecration to be natural. While I was living in this way, one summer I saw a great crowd of men, Egyptians and Libyans, going down toward the sea. I stopped one of them and asked him where they were going in such haste. He told me, "They are all going to Jerusalem for the Exaltation of the Holy Cross which is to be celebrated there in a few days time." Then I said to him, "Do you think they would take me, if I wanted to go with them?" "Anyone who has the fare can go" he replied. I said, "Indeed, brother, I have neither the fare nor any food, but I will go and get into one of the ships that are going and they will take me even if they do not want to. I have a body and that will serve as both fare and food for me." For I wanted to go (forgive me, my father) so that I might soon have more lovers for my lust.

Cap. XIV. 'I beg you, my lord and father, do not force me to say any more about my shame, for I am afraid of the judgement of God and lest my words corrupt both you and the very air.' Then Zossima, watering the ground with tears, said to her, 'For God's sake, speak, Mother; go on and do not break the thread of your life-giving narrative.' So she took up the story again and continued: 'Then the young man who had heard my obscene remarks went away, laughing. I threw away the spindle that I was carrying (for until then I used to have it with me) and I ran down to the sea, whither I had seen the others hurrying; I saw some young men, about ten in number, standing on the shore, with beautiful bodies and graceful movements, and I judged them just right for what I wanted. They were waiting, it seemed, for the rest of their sailing companions, while some had already gone ahead into the ship. So as was my custom, I shamelessly pushed into the midst of them and said, "Take me wherever you are going

and I will not be without my uses for you." I added more and
more shameless things and they were all moved to laughter.
When they saw that I was ready for anything shameless, they
accepted me and carried me into their ship which was ready to
sail, and we set sail at once. How can I tell you, man of God,
about what followed? What tongue can say, what ear can hear
what happened on that ship and during that voyage, for I
compelled into sin even those who were unwilling. There
was no kind of perverted and unspeakable lust that I did not
perform with them. I am amazed, my father, that the sea carried my lusts and that the earth did not open to take me alive
down into hell. But I think my God was seeking my repentance, for He does not desire the death of sinners (1 Tim. 2)
but guards them in His loving kindness, waiting for them to
be converted (Ezek. 18). So I continued in this way until we
reached Jerusalem and for all the days there that preceded the
festival, I was occupied in similar or even worse behaviour. I
was not content to have had the young men with whom I had
satisfied my lusts at sea during the voyage, but misused
others on land, both the citizens and those who were there as
pilgrims.

Cap. XV. 'Now when the festival of the Exaltation of the
Precious Cross came round, and I was going about as usual
hunting for the souls of young men, I saw at first light that
everyone was going to the church. So I went along, running
with those who were running there and I came with them
into the forecourt of the cathedral. At the hour for the Exaltation of the Holy Cross I pushed and was pushed, fighting
my way fiercely through the crowd to get in. So somehow, I,
unhappy wretch that I was, came near to where the life-
giving wood was being displayed. But as soon as I reached
the threshold where others were going in without difficulty, I
was prevented from entering by a kind of force. I was pushed
back and found myself standing alone in the courtyard. I
thought it had only happened because of my weakness as a
woman, so again I mingled with the others, struggling and
using my elbows to push forward to the same spot; but I
laboured in vain.

Cap. XVI. All the rest went in without difficulty, with no
impediment, but as soon as I set foot on the threshold of the

church, it refused to admit me. It was as if a detachment of soldiers stood in the way to prevent me from entering; some unexplained power repelled me and I stood again in the fore-court. I suffered this again three or four times and at last, worn out, I gave up pushing and being pushed back (for I lacked strength of body for such violence). I drew back and stood in a corner of the forecourt. And only then did I begin to see why it was that I was being prevented from going in to see the life-giving wood. For a salutary understanding touched my mind and the eyes of my heart and shewed me that it was the sinfulness of my actions that prevented me from going in. So I began to weep and grieve and beat my breast; I drew sighs and tears from the bottom of my heart. And then I saw in the place where I was standing, a picture of the holy Mother of God. Gazing directly into her eyes, I said, "Virgin and Lady, who gave birth to the Word of God according to the flesh, I see now that it is not suitable or decent for me, defiled as I am, to look upon this picture of you, ever immaculate Virgin, who always kept your body and soul chaste and clean from all sin. Indeed, it would be right for you in your purity to reject and loathe my impurity. But God to whom you gave birth became man, as I have heard, to save sinners and to call them to repentance; so help me, for I am alone and without any other help. Receive my confession, and give me leave to enter the church and do not deprive me of the sight of that most precious wood upon which was fixed God made man, whom you carried and bore as a Virgin and where He gave His blood for my redemption. O Lady, let the doors be opened to me so that I may adore the divine cross. I beg you, from whom Christ took flesh, to guarantee my promise, which is, that I will never again defile my flesh by immersing it in horrifying lusts. As soon as I have seen the cross of your Son, holy Virgin, I will go where-ever you as my mediator for salvation shall order and lead."

Cap. XVII. 'When I had said this, with burning faith, as if receiving some assurance from some sure source, and trust-ing in the mercy of heart of the Mother of God, I moved out of the place in which I had been standing to pray, and once more I mingled with those who were going in. There was nothing to push me away or prevent me from approaching

the door by which they were going into church. At that point
a great terror and stupor came over me, and I trembled all
over, but when I came to the door which until then had been
closed to me, it was as if all the force that had previously prevented me from entering now allowed me to go in. So I was
admitted without hindrance, and went into the holy of holies
and I was found worthy to worship the mystery of the
precious and life-giving Wood of the Cross. Thus I understood the promises of God and realised how God receives
those who repent. I threw myself on the floor and kissed the
sacred dust. Then I went out and ran back to her who was my
mediator. I came to the place where I had set my signature to
the promise I had made to her who guaranteed it and kneeling
before the face of Mother of God, ever Virgin. I spoke thus:
"O most loving Lady, you have always shown merciful
loving-kindness; you have not rejected the prayer of an
unworthy sinner. I have gazed upon that Glory which was
rightly kept from the sight of the impure; glory to God, who
accepts through You the repentance of sinners. What more
can I, a sinner, think or say? It is time, Lady, to keep the
pledge which I made with you as my witness and to fulfil that
which I promised. Now therefore, lead me wherever you
please; lead me to salvation, teach me what is true, and go
before me in the way of repentance." When I had said this, I
heard a voice far off which said, "If you cross over the Jordan,
you will find rest." When I heard the voice say this, I believed
it had come because of me, and I cried out, weeping, towards
the picture of the Mother of God, "Lady, Lady, Queen of the
whole world, by whom salvation came to the human race, do
not forsake me." When I had said this, I went out of the courtyard of the church and at once I hurried away. As I went,
someone noticed me and gave me three pennies, saying,
"Take these, mother". So I took them and bought three
loaves with them, receiving them as a blessing for my journey. I asked the man who sold me the bread, "Where is the
road to the Jordan and what is it like?" When I was shown the
city gates which lead in that direction, I ran out of them,
weeping, and set out on my journey.

Cap. XVIII. I asked the way from those whom I met and
walked for the rest of the day. It had been the third hour (i.e. 9

o'clock) when I deserved to see the precious and holy Cross. At sunset I saw the Church of St John the Baptist near the Jordan, and having prayed in the church, I went down immediately to the Jordan and washed my hands and face in its holy water. Then I made my communion of the most pure and life-giving Sacrament of Christ the Lord, in the Church of St John, Forerunner and Baptist; I ate half a loaf and drank from the Jordan; all night I lay on the ground. At first light, I crossed over to the other side and again I begged my Guide to lead me wherever she pleased. So I came into this desert and from that time until this day, I go further and run on, waiting for my God who saves those who turn to Him out of faintness of heart and in tempest' (Ps. 54). Zossima asked her, 'How many years have passed, my Lady, since you began to live in the desert?' The woman replied, 'I think it is forty-seven years since I left the holy city.' Zossima asked her, 'And what have you been able to find to eat, my lady?' The woman replied. 'I was carrying two and a half loaves when I crossed the Jordan, and after a while they became hard as stones and I have gone on eating a little of them at a time for all these years.' Then Zossima said, 'And have you passed this length of time without suffering? Have you felt nothing of the violence of this sudden change?' She said, 'Now you are asking me about something which I tremble to speak of, if I am to remember what great dangers I have borne and the evil thoughts that confused me. For I am afraid lest I suffer more tribulation from them again.' Zossima said, 'Lady, hide nothing from me. Let us speak clearly for once about this in order to learn what we ought.'

Cap. XIX. So she said to him, 'Believe me, father, I struggled for seventeen years with the wild beasts of huge and irrational desires; when I began to eat, my desire was for meat; I longed for the fish that they have in Egypt, I even desired the wine which had been so sweet to me; for I had enjoyed wine very much and I used to drink so much that I got drunk; and now I craved that which I had used so much in the world. But here I did not even have water when I was burning in the heat and in very great need. Also there came to me a great longing for songs of a lewd kind, troubling me and making me remember the devilish songs I had learned to sing

in the world. At once then weeping and beating my breast I
brought back to my mind the promise of faithfulness which I
had made when I entered this solitude. In imagination, I
would come before the picture of the Holy Mother of God,
who had accepted me on trust, and implore her to chase from
me those thoughts which were afflicting my most wretched
soul. So when I had wept greatly and grievously, beating my
breast courageously, I saw a light which shone around me on
every side and soon I became calm and safe. As for the
thoughts that would push me into harlotry again, I do not
know, Father; how can I tell you about those? When such
thoughts grew in me, I would fling myself on the ground and
flood the earth with weeping, hoping that She would stand
by me who had been my guarantor, appearing to me in my
disobedience and threatening me with punishment for my
crimes. I did not get up from the ground until that most sweet
light shone around me and drove away the thoughts raging in
me. Often I directed the eyes of my heart to her, my guarantor, praying to her without ceasing to help me in this solitude
to repentance. For I have her as my helper whose purity bore
our Creator. And so for seventeen years, as I told you, I lived
among many dangers, until now. From that time till this, my
helper the Mother of God has been with me, and she directs
me in all things.' Then Zossima said, 'You had no food or
clothing?' And she replied, 'As I told you, I used up the loaves
seventeen years ago, and then I ate herbs that I found in the
desert. The clothing that I had when I crossed over Jordan
tore and fell to pieces with age. I endured much from the
freezing of cold and the burning of heat: I was burned by the
heat of summer and frozen stiff and shivering in the winter by
so much cold; often I fell to the ground and lay there unmov-
ing, without breath, struggling with many and diverse needs
and huge temptations but through it all even until this day the
power of God has guarded my unhappy soul and body. When
I think from what evils the Lord has freed me, I am nourished
by incorruptible food, and I cover my shoulders with the
hope of my salvation. I feed upon and cover myself with the
Word of God, who contains all things (Deut. 8). For man
does not live by bread alone (Matt. 11.44) and all who have no
clothing will be clothed in stone having discarded the outer

covering of sins (Job 24; Zech. 3.1–10; Is. 61.10).

Cap. XX. When Zossima heard how she drew her witnesses from the Scriptures, from the books of Moses and Job, with the Psalms, he said to her, 'Have you learned the psalms, then, mother, and read the other books of Holy Scripture?' When she heard this she smiled and said to him, 'Believe me, I have seen no one since I crossed over Jordan until I saw you today, not even an animal or any kind of creature since I came into this desert. Never in any way did I learn letters nor have I ever heard anyone reading or singing them, but the Word of God living and active itself teaches man knowledge (Heb. 4.12). That is enough about me. Now I ask you, by the Incarnation of God the Word, to pray to the Lord for me, a sinner.' When she had said this, the old man ran to her and knelt at her feet, weeping and saying, 'Blessed be the Lord God who does great and wonderful things, glorious and marvellous, without end (John 10). You are indeed blessed, O God, for you have shown me how generous you are to those who fear you. O Lord, you do not abandon those who seek you' (Ps. 9). She restrained the old man and would not let him bow right down but said to him 'I implore you, sir, by our Lord and Saviour, Jesus Christ, tell no one anything you have heard until God releases me from this flesh. Now you have heard all this, go in peace, and this time next year I will show myself again to you, and you will see me, if God preserves us. And for the Lord's sake, do what I am going to ask: when the holy season of fasting comes round next year, do not cross the Jordan as is usually done in that monastery.' Zossima was astonished to hear her talking to him about the custom of the monastery as if she knew it, but he said nothing except to glorify God who gives great things to those who love him. Then she said, 'Stay in the monastery, father, as I have told you, and even if you want to go out, you will not be able to do so. But at sunset on the most holy day of the Lord's Supper, take for me a portion of the life-giving Body and Blood in a holy vessel, worthy of such mysteries, and bring it to me on the bank of Jordan, on the inhabited side, so that when I come I may receive the life-giving gifts. Since the time when I made my communion in the church of the most blessed Forerunner before crossing the Jordan, never have I received those

holy things, and so I implore you not to refuse my request:
bring me the life-giving and divine mysteries at that hour
when the Lord made His disciples partakers of the holy
Supper. And I send this message to Father John, the abbot of
the monastery in which you live: look to yourself and to your
flock; something is happening there that needs correction. I
do not want you to tell him about this now but when the Lord
directs you to do so.' With these words, she asked him to pray
for her, and disappeared very swiftly into the depths of the
desert.

Cap. XXI. As for Zossima, he fell on his knees and kissed
the ground on which her feet had stood, giving glory to God.
Then with great thankfulness he went away, praising and
blessing our Lord and God, Jesus Christ. He passed through
the desert again and returned to the monastery on the very
day when the monks returned there. He remained silent all
the year, not daring to tell anyone what he had seen but by
himself he prayed to God that He would show him again the
face he longed to see. He sighed to think how slowly a year
goes by. When the Sunday came which starts the holy fast, at
once everyone went out into the desert with customary
prayers and singing of psalms. But Zossima was kept back, ill
with a fever, and remained in the monastery. And he remembered that the Holy One had told him that even if he wanted
to go out of the monastery, he would not be able to do so.
Some days passed and he got up after his illness but stayed in
the monastery. When the monks returned and the day came
for the Holy Supper, he did what he had been told to do and
took in a small chalice a portion of the precious Body and
Blood of Christ our God, and he put figs and dates in a basket
with some lentils soaked in water. He left late in the evening
and sat down on the bank of the Jordan to wait for the Holy
One to come. When the Holy Woman was late, Zossima did
not fall asleep but watched the desert closely, waiting to see
that for which he longed. Then he said to himself, 'Perhaps
she has already been and not finding me, gone back?' And
saying this, he began to weep, raising his eyes to heaven and
praying to God, saying, 'Do not send me away, O Lord,
without seeing that which you once allowed me to behold.'

Cap. XXII. While he was praying and weeping in this way,

another thought struck him: 'What will happen if she does come? How will she cross the Jordan since there is no boat? How can she come to me, unworthy as I am? Alas, I am wretched; who is keeping such beauty from me?' The old man was turning these things over in his mind, when lo, the Holy One came, and stood on the other bank from whence she had come. When Zossima saw her, he arose rejoicing and greatly exulting he glorified God. And again the thought seized him that she could not cross the Jordan, but when he looked he saw her signing the waters of the Jordan with the sign of the Cross. For the darkness was lit by the full splendour of the moon, since it was that time in the month. As soon as she had made the sign of the Cross, she stepped on to the water and walking over the flowing waves she came as if walking on solid land. Zossima was amazed and began to kneel, but she stopped him, calling over the water and saying, 'What are you doing, father, you who are a priest of God and carrying the holy mysteries?' At once he obeyed her words. When she came up from the water, she said to the old man, 'Give me a blessing, father, give me a blessing.' He replied with great haste, (for a great stupor had come over him at so glorious a miracle) and said, 'Indeed God does not lie when he promises that we shall be like him, insofar as we have been purified. Glory to you, Christ our God, who have shown me by your handmaiden here how much I should consider myself below the measure of true perfection.' When he had said this the woman asked him to say the Holy Creed and then he began the Lord's Prayer. When he had finished the Our Father, the Holy One, as is the custom, gave the kiss of peace to the old man. And then she received the life-giving gifts of the sacrament, groaning and weeping with her hands held up to heaven, she cried out, 'Lord, now let your servant depart in peace, according to your word; for my eyes have seen your salvation' (Luke 2.29). And she said to the old man, 'Forgive me, father, and fulfil my other wish: go now to the monastery and may the peace of God keep you. Return in a year to the stream where I first met you. Do not fail me in this but for God's sake, come. It is the will of God that you see me again.' He answered her, 'Would that it were possible now to follow your footsteps and have the precious fruit of the sight

of your face! Tarry, mother, grant a little request of an old
man and deign to accept a little food which I have brought.'
Saying this he showed her the basket he had brought with
him. She touched the lentils with the tip of her finger and
taking three grains placed them in her mouth, saying that the
grace of the Holy Spirit is sufficient to keep whole the substance of the soul. Then she said to the old man, 'For God's
sake pray for me, and remember me always as a sinner.' He
touched the feet of the Holy One and with tears begged her to
pray for the Church, for the Kingdom and for himself and so,
weeping, he let her go, for he would not detain her any longer
if she did not will it.

Cap. XXIII. So once again she made the sign of the Cross
over the Jordan and crossed over, walking on the element of
water in the same way that she had when she came. And the
old man went back full of joy and fear, reproaching himself
that he had not asked the holy one her name; but he hoped to
do so the following year.

Cap. XXIV. So when a year had again passed, he went
again into the huge solitude of the desert, having done everything according to custom, and he hurried towards that marvellous sight. He walked through the desert without finding
any indications that this was the place he was looking for, so
he looked right and left, turning his gaze in all directions as if
he were a huntsman wanting to capture a much coveted
animal. But seeing no movement anywhere he began to weep
bitterly. And looking up to heaven he began to pray, 'Shew
me, O Lord, that angel in the flesh of whom the world is not
worthy.'

Cap. XXV. Having prayed in this way, he came to the
place which looked like a stream and on the other side he saw
the rising sun, and when he looked, he saw the Holy One
lying dead, her hands folded and her face turned to the East.
Running up to her, he watered the feet of the blessed one with
tears; otherwise he did not dare to touch her. He wept for
some time and said the appropriate psalms, then the prayer
for the dead, and then he said to himself, 'Is it right to bury
the holy body here?' And then he saw by her head these words
written in the earth: 'Father Zossima, bury in this place the
body of Mary the sinner, return me to the earth of which I am

made, dust to dust, having prayed to the Lord for me, who died on the first day of the Egyptian month of Pharmuti called the fifth of the Ides of April by the Romans, on the self-same night as the Passion of the Lord after making her communion of the Divine and Mysterious Supper.'

Cap. XXVI. When he had read what was written, the old man wondered who it was that had written those words, since she had told him that she was unlettered, but he rejoiced to know the name of the Holy One. He realised that as soon as she had received communion from the divine mysteries by the Jordan, in that same hour she had come to the place where at once she had passed from this world. The same journey which had taken Zossima twenty days with difficulty, Mary had covered in an hour and then at once passed on to God. So Zossima glorified God and shed tears on the body, saying, 'It is time, Zossima, to fulfil the command. But how, wretched man, are you going to dig out a grave with nothing but your hands?' Then he saw not far away a small piece of wood, thrown down in the desert. Picking it up he set about digging. But the ground was dry and very hard, and would not yield to the efforts of the old man. He grew tired, and poured with sweat. He sighed from the depths of his soul and raising his eyes he saw a great lion standing by the body of the Holy One and licking her feet. When he saw the lion he trembled with fear, especially because he remembered that Mary had said she had never met any animals. But protecting himself with the sign of the cross, he believed that he would be kept from harm by the power of the One who lay there. As for the lion, it walked up to him, expressing friendliness in every movement. Zossima said to the lion, 'Greatest of the beasts, you have been sent by God, so that the body of the Holy One should be buried, for I am old and have not enough strength to dig her grave. I have no spade and I cannot go back all that distance to fetch suitable tools. So do the work with your paws and we shall be able to give to the earth the mortal tabernacle of the saint.'

Cap. XXVII. 'While he was still speaking the lion had already dug out with its front paws a hole big enough to bury the body in. Again the old man watered the feet of the Holy One with tears and then, with the lion standing by, he called upon her to pray for everyone, he covered her body with earth; it was naked as it had been before, except for the torn monastic cloak which Zossima had thrown across her and with which Mary, turning away, had partially covered her body. Then they both withdrew. The lion went off into the depths of the desert as meekly if it were a lamb, and Zossima went home, blessing and praising God and singing hymns of praise to our Lord Christ. When he reached the monastery, he told the monks everything that he had heard and seen, hiding nothing. From the very beginning he told them everything in detail and all marvelled to hear of God's wonders and kept the memory of the saint in fear and love. As for abbot John, he did find a few in the monastery in need of correction, so that none of the saint's words proved useless or inexplicable. Zossima lived in that monastery until he was a hundred, and then he went in peace to God, thanks be to our Lord Jesus Christ, who with the Father is one in power and honour and glory, with the adorable and life-giving Spirit, now and for-ever and to the ages of ages, amen.

(The monks preserved this story without writing it down, and offered it to anyone who wanted to hear it as a pattern for edification, but no one had heard of anyone writing it down to this day. But I have told in writing what I heard orally. Per-haps others also have described the life of the saint and much better and more worthily than I have, but this has not come to my notice. As far as lies in my power, I have written down this account, putting truth before everything else. And may God who gives great things to those who seek him, grant benefit to those who read this story, as a reward for the one he ordered to write it. And may he deign to accept him into that same company and assembly where dwells that blessed Mary about whom this story is, together with all those who throughout the generations have pleased him with godly thoughts and labours. And let us all glorify God, King of all generations, that he may vouchsafe his mercy to us also at the day of Judgement in Christ Jesus our Lord, to whom is due all glory, honour and worship together with the Father without beginning, now and forever and to the ages of ages. AMEN.

CHAPTER FOUR

Pelagia; Beauty Riding By

*But the most blessed Nonnus gazed after her very in-
tently, for a very long time, and after she had gone by he
turned round and still gazed after her: then he turned
towards the bishops sitting round him and said, 'Were
you not delighted by such great beauty?'*[1]

The story of Mary Magdalene was known through the
gospels, the story of Mary of Egypt through the liturgy; they
belong to the whole church and through them the central
truth of salvation for sinners is offered to all. There is a pro-
found connection between these stories and the theme in the
Bible of the harlot as image of unfaithful Israel, but with the
image there is also the fact of actual persons who lived as prostitutes; that is, offering sexual intercourse indiscriminately,
and usually as a commercial transaction, and who then turned
from this way of life to Christ and the life of the Kingdom.
Their conversion is presented as especially striking, and is
therefore meant to bring the hope of salvation to all sinners,
whatever form their alienation from God has taken; if these
women can be saved, these stories affirm, so can everyone.

It is not surprising, therefore, to find that such stories were
of special interest to monks, whose whole life was pre-
eminently concerned with sin and conversion. These stories
were told and retold in monastic circles in Egypt and
Palestine from the fourth century onwards and formed part of
the written literature of the *apophthegmata* and the *vitae
patrum*. They are stories of dramatic sin and equally vivid conversion, set in the monastic world of the deserts of Egypt and
Palestine. Three among them were especially elaborated and
presented as a well-known set of texts, along with the *Life of
Mary of Egypt* and, at times, with accounts of Mary of Mag-

dala.[2] These are the stories of the *meretrices*; Pelagia the actress
of Antioch, Thaïs the harlot, and Maria the niece of Abraham. Such accounts were deliberately used as a balance to the
accounts of the lives of the good women of the monastic
world, such as Marcella[3], Eugenia[4], Macrina[5], and Melania.[6]
Each of the harlots was involved in commercial transactions
about sex, from which each was set free to live on the heights
of ascetic love and prayer. Such accounts provided a stimulus
and an encouragement for all christians, but especially for
monks.

Each of these texts has a complex history, and, as with
Mary Magdalene and Mary of Egypt, literary figures emerge
from the story of Pelagia which are perhaps not identical with
the historical person's who gave rise to the tales. They are not
merely biographies but stories, told in order to present fundamental truths in a lively and accessible narrative form. So successful were they, that they have continued to gain the
attention of people outside as well as within the monastic
milieu in all ages, from the monks of Egypt in the fourth century to Anatole France and Helen Waddell; they have been
retold; they have formed the inspiration for music, poetry
and art and even for the cartoon in Northern Europe. When
Humbert of Romans, the master of the Order of Preachers,
prepared a book of pattern sermons for the use of friars, he included one based on the lives of Mary Magdalene, Mary of
Egypt, and Pelagia, in which he could assume at least an ac-
quaintance with all three stories among both the friars and
their audience:

> Now there are three things which make for greatness in
> repentance, that is, great grief for the past, great caution
> for the future, and great works of repentance now. The
> first was evident from the abundant tears which were in
> them, as befell the Magdalene, Mary of Egypt and St
> Pelagia when they looked at what they had done. The
> second was evident in their actions, for after her conver-
> sion, the Magdalene was always in association with the
> Lord or His disciples or she was in the cave where she
> remained for thirty years; Mary of Egypt at once went
> into the desert after her conversion in which she was un-
> known to the world for forty years; St Pelagia after her

conversion fled secretly to become a recluse disguised as a monk. Thirdly, how much they suffered from fasting and harshness and vigils and so on can be read about in the accounts of their lives aforementioned.[7]

He also goes on to mention the harlot Thaïs, and declares that they all entered heaven at death, which, he says, is an example of the results of receiving mercy and forgiveness, and he supports his affirmation with two quotations from the Bible which were connected with these stories from the first:

> It is a great confusion to many that harlots, foul with the mire of their sins, go first onto the kingdom: 'Amen I say unto you, the harlots go before you into the kingdom of God' (Matt.21); 'Where sin abounded grace did much more abound' (Rom.5).[8]

The first of these stories, that of the harlot Pelagia as told by the deacon James of Edessa, is memorable among any collection of tales. Helen Waddell suggests that, simply because it was supremely well told, it had been retold less often than the other stories, 'already in the first paragraph one knows oneself in the hands of a great novelist'.[9] Pelagia was a well-known actress in Antioch, and therefore belonged, in the eyes of the Church, to a class of immoral persons which included jesters, mimics, jongleurs, clowns, as well as prostitutes. One day she passed along the road, beautifully, if scantily, dressed, riding with her lively young companions and servants and with music and laughter. They passed close by a group of christian bishops who were holding a conference in the open air. The bishops, the story says, hid their faces from the sight, but bishop Nonnus, a monk-bishop from the desert[10], 'did long and most intently regard her and after she had passed by, still he gazed and his eyes went after her.' Then, turning his head, he looked at the bishops and said, 'did not her great beauty delight you? Indeed, it delighted me' (p. 67). This recognition of the beauty of Pelagia as a creature formed by God struck Nonnus to the heart; a man of genuine prayer, he was able to see her truly while the more timid men, who were aware of their own capacity for lust, hid their eyes.

Nonnus then drew a parallel for his companions between

the courtesan, who spent all her time on her appearance to please her lovers, and the tepid christian who can spare only a small part of the day to make his soul beautiful for Christ, the great lover of souls. Later, however, when he was alone, his heartfelt wonder at the beauty he had seen returned. He prayed for Pelagia with such force that James, his deacon and his Boswell, was afraid and hid.

Next day, Pelagia heard Nonnus preaching and was moved to repentance. She wrote to him and then came to him and begged for baptism at his hands. Once baptised, she secretly asked Nonnus for men's clothing and fled by night, only the two of them knowing her plans. Years later, when James the Deacon was going to visit Palestine, Nonnus told him to visit a hermit there called Pelagius. When James found the cell of the solitary, he discovered that the inmate had just died, venerated throughout the country for austerity and prayer; the hermit was Pelagia.

Like the written account of Mary of Egypt, the story of Pelagia has many counterparts and sources[11], but the story, as it stands in the account of the deacon James, provided food for meditation for centuries. Two themes in particular were of interest in the monastic tradition: first, there is the use of the image of the courtesan used as a rebuke to the life of the monk; and secondly there is the story of the hidden hermit who is known after death to have been a woman.

The idea of using the image of the courtesan as a rebuke or example to monks was not new with Nonnus; it is found in many other texts. For instance, in two passages in the *Sayings of the Desert Fathers*, John the Dwarf, as has been said, compares the soul to a courtesan.[12] A second passage attributed to him on the same theme is even more startling and enigmatic than the first:

> One of the old men said, 'John you are like a courtesan who shews her beauty to increase the number of her lovers.' Abba John kissed him and said, 'you are quite right, father'.[13]

A saying attributed to Abba Pambo is closer to the use made by Nonnus of the sight of Pelagia:

Athanasius the archbishop of Alexandria of holy memory, begged Abba Pambo to come down from the desert to Alexandria. He went down and seeing an actress, he began to weep. Those who were present asked him the reason for his tears and he said, 'Two things make me weep: one is the loss of the woman; and the other is that I am not so concerned to please God as she is to please wicked men'.[14]

In another story, this time from an Armenian source, the prostitute herself rebukes a desert father and draws the moral:

When Ephraim went into Edessa for the first time, he prayed to God that as he entered the town he would meet someone who would discuss with him the problems in Holy Scripture. The first person he met, coming straight towards him, was a woman who was a prostitute. Ephraim was sad because he thought God had not heard his prayer, for what did she know of the Bible? How could she help resolve his questions? But the woman came on, her eyes fixed upon him. He was astonished and said to her, but without impatience or anger, 'Why are you looking at me so intently?' The woman replied with a reference to the story in Genesis of the creation of man and woman, 'It is natural that I should look at you, for I was formed out of you; but as for you, you have no reason to look at me for it was the earth from which you were formed and it is on that that your eyes should be fixed'.[15]

In this story, as in others, the prostitute is shown as lively and intelligent, with a knowledge of the scriptures; Pelagia is someone who takes it as a matter of course that she will send a letter to the bishop. But the main point of the re-telling of such stories in the desert is to bring home to the individual his state as a sinner, unfaithful to God, and not giving as much care to his soul as a prostitute does to her clothes. There is, here, the biblical precedent of the prophets who described Israel as a prostitute, unfaithful to God by loving other gods, and with no care for keeping the commandments of the one who loves her. The contrast between prostitute and monk is here reversed from what would be expected about each.

The second theme (also well known in the desert) in this story of Pelagia is that of the woman who disguises herself as a man, in order to live the life of a hermit, secretly until her death. In the story of Mary of Egypt and the related text about the Virgin of Jerusalem, it is at first assumed by the visitors who see the reformed prostitutes in the desert that they are men, and they are all the more astonished to discover that this extreme of asceticism has been undertaken by women. In the *Sayings of the Desert Fathers* a story of this kind is told of abba Bessarion; it is related by his disciple, Doulas:

> We walked on and came to a cave where we found a brother seated, engaged in plaiting a rope. He did not raise his eyes to us or greet us, since he did not want to enter into conversation with us . . . On our return, we came again to the cave where we had seen the brother. The old man said to me, 'Let us go in and see him; perhaps God has told him to speak to us'. When we had entered we found him dead. The old man said to me, 'Come, brother, let us take the body; it is for this reason that God has sent us here.' When we took the body to bury it, we perceived that it was a woman. Filled with astonishment, the old man said, 'See how the women triumph over Satan while we still behave badly in the towns.'[16]

The assumption of male dress points to the very practical need for a woman living alone in desert to protect herself. But there is more to it than that. The way to have a place in the world of early monasticism was to transcend gender differences either by life in a single sex community, or by undertaking a solitary form of life in which it was more prudent, for example in the desert where there were hostile marauders, for a woman to dress as a man. Either way opened the path of return, for men and for women, to the paradisal state of unfallen Adam, or rather, the heaven of the new Adam, where 'there is neither male nor female' (Gal. 3.28). However, an exception to this pattern of withdrawal suggests that a change of dress was neither universal nor fundamental: amma Sarah lived alone by the Nile for sixty years without wearing male attire or joining a convent of nuns. She says that for the first thirteen she had to fight daily against the demon of lust, and it is significant that she dealt with this in exactly the same way as the other hermits; 'she never prayed that the warfare should cease but she said O Lord give me strength for the fight'.[17] Two remarks of hers show how deeply she felt her equality with men in monastic life to be, which went much deeper than details of dress: she said, 'according to my nature I am a woman but not according to my thoughts'[18], and to some visiting monks she said, 'It is I who am a man, you who are women'.[19]

The idea of 'becoming a man' through undertaking monastic life is connected with the freedom offered to women by Christianity itself. Life in the desert, *anachoreisis*, was a practical demonstration of freedom from the limitations and responsibilities of society. It seems that it was very often the wealthy women of the ancient world who were able to take advantage of the desert as an arena of freedom. The women who had been harlots were rich women; Pelagia had a household of servants to provide for and her name in the city was 'Margaret', a pearl, because of her beauty but also because of her wealth in jewels. By their successful careers they had achieved a freedom from the control of father or husband, and from the domesticity inevitable for a woman of good reputation. Like the great widows of Rome, Paula, Melania and Macrina, they were both free and rich; and the further stage of that freedom was to enter the monastic world of the desert where gender was, by definition, of no significance at all. Prudent and wise, aware of the strength of both sexuality and the pull of the hearth for men and for themselves, these women took care not to present themselves in any way as a female. This has nothing to do with a rejection of femininity; in fact it was an assertion of it; before God, all souls are feminine, and it is this femininity that the women claim, as do the men of the desert.[20]

In examining the story of Nonnus and Pelagia there is another aspect which deserves comment; that is, the relationship of love between them. It is interesting to note that, before the story begins, they had never heard of one another: it was indeed a matter of 'love at first sight'. Nonnus was at a meeting of bishops when he first saw Pelagia, and his immediate reaction was astonished wonder at her beauty.

Pelagia did not notice him then but later, when she entered a church by chance and as soon as she heard Nonnus preaching, she was moved by wonder and trust; at once she made personal contact with him and insisted that he himself should be personally responsible for her baptism. Their immediate appreciation of one another is shown in these two moments of encounter – Nonnus sees her riding by; Pelagia hears his words in church. The delicate theme of the love between them pervades the account as seen through the amazed eyes of James the Deacon. It was a love so strong that at first Nonnus could not trust himself to hear Pelagia's confession and baptise her; and later, Pelagia, knowing the strength of desire, planned with him that she should leave at once, secretly, for the solitude of the desert. They never met again, but neither forgot the other, and Nonnus knew where she was living. It was a love purified and strengthened by parting; and at the end they exchanged greetings before their entry into the Kingdom.

There are other stories of great love in the desert, but they are rare. One is told in a collection of anonymous stories by abba Simeon about his own life: he had been a trader in Syria and when his partner died, he wanted to marry his widow since he loved her very much:

> She, moved by his youth and beauty ... said to him, 'By God, I believe that you love no-one more than me?' He said to her, 'It is so'. She said to him, 'I, and this is God's truth, also love you but since it is the voice of the Lord which says, "If someone comes to me and does not hate his father and mother and wife and children and brothers and even his own life he cannot be my disciple (Lk.14.26)" let us part from one another because of God'.[21]

In the same collection of *Sayings* there are other stories of monks deterred from sexual encounter by the woman they approached[22], and here, also, the woman is presented, not as a temptress, but as a wise and far-sighted person, acting according to God in a fraught situation. But these are not stories about relationship and affection. In the stories of Mary of Egypt and Zossima, of Thaïs and Paphnutius, and, in a different way, in that of Mari and Abraham, a relationship of genuine and warm love forms part of the way of redemption. What is unusual in the story of Pelagia and Nonnus is the equality of love between the two, and their very positive appreciation of each other which is fulfilled, and in no way denied, by their choice of chastity and solitude.

NOTES TO CHAPTER FOUR

The text used here is *Vita Sanctae Pelagiae, Meretricis* in PL 73, cols. 663–72. For a full discussion of the texts see *Pélagie la pénitente: Métamorphoses d'une Légende*, Tom.1, *Les Textes et leur histoire* (Paris, 1981).

The text is also printed in Acta SS, Oct. IV, 261–6. (*BHL* 6605.) There is an English translation in Helen Waddell, *The Desert Fathers* (London, 1936), pp. 267–81

1. pp. 66–75.
2. e.g. PL 73, cols. 651–90.
3. Jerome, *Vita Sanctae Marcellae*, PL 22, cols. 1087–95. (*BHL* 5222.)
4. *Vita Sanctae Eugeniae*, PL 73, cols. 602–24. (*BHL* 2666.)
5. Gregory of Nyssa, *Vita Macrinae Junioris*, PG 46, cols. 959–1000.
6. Palladius, *Vita Melania Senior*, PL 74, cols. 318–20.
7. Humbert of Romans, *De Eruditione Praedicatorum*, Pt. 2, iv, 20 (I am indebted to Fr Simon Tugwell O.P. for allowing me to translate from his transcription.)
8. *ibid.*
9. Helen Waddell, *The Desert Fathers* (London, 1936), p. 262.
10. Nonnus: mentioned in the Roman martyrology for 2 December.
11. cf. *Pélagie la Pénitente, op. cit.*
12. *Sayings*, John the Dwarf 16; see page 96.
13. *ibid.* 46.
14. *ibid.* Pambo 4.
15. *Vita S. Ephraem*, PL 73, cols. 2321–22.
16. *Sayings*, Bessarion 3.
17. *ibid.* Sarah 1.
18. *ibid.* 4.
19. *ibid.* 9.

20. cf. 'Apophthegmata Matrem', B. Ward, in *Studia Patristica*, vol. 16 (Berlin, 1985), pp. 63–6.
21. *World*, p. 16.
22. *ibid*. pp. 14 and 15.

English translation of the *Life of Saint Pelagia the Harlot* written by the Deacon James and translated into Latin by Eustochius.

Verse Prologue by Eustocius.

> The words of this writer about holy hidden things
> Have I, Eustochius, into Latin rendered;
> Good readers, take note of all my labour,
> And ask God in your prayers to remember me.

Preface of the Author. We should always have in mind the great mercy of our Lord who does not will the death of sinners but rather that all should be converted to repentance and live (1 Tim. 2). So, listen to a wonder that happened in our times. It has seemed good to me, James, to write this to you, holy brothers, so that by hearing or reading it you may gain the greatest possible aid for your souls. For the merciful God, who wills that no one should perish, has given us these days for the forgiveness of our sins, since in the time to come He will judge justly and reward everyone according to his works. Now be silent, and listen to me with all the care of which you are capable because what I have to tell you is very rich in compunction for us all.

Cap. I. The most holy bishop of the city of Antioch called together all the bishops nearby about a certain matter; and so eight bishops came, and among them was Nonnus, the most holy man of God, my bishop, a marvellous man and a most observant monk of the monastery called Tabennisis. Because of his incomparable life and most excellent conduct, he had been snatched away from the monastery and ordained bishop. When we had all assembled in the aforesaid city, the bishop of Antioch told us the meeting would be in the church of the most blessed martyr Julianus. So we went out and sat there before the door of the church with the other bishops who had come.

Cap. II. When we were seated, the bishops asked my lord

Nonnus to speak to them, and at once the holy bishop began to speak words for the edification and salvation of all. Now while we were marvelling at his holy teaching, lo, suddenly there came among us the chief actress of Antioch, the first in the chorus in the theatre, sitting on a donkey. She was dressed in the height of fantasy, wearing nothing but gold, pearls and precious stones, even her bare feet were covered with gold and pearls. With her went a great throng of boys and girls all dressed in cloth of gold with collars of gold on their necks, going before and following her. So great was her beauty that all the ages of mankind could never come to the end of it. So they passed through our company, filling all the air with traces of music and the most sweet smell of perfume. When the bishops saw her bare-headed and with all her limbs shamelessly exposed with such lavish display, there was not one who did not hide his face in his veil or his scapular, averting their eyes as if from a very great sin.

Cap. III. But the most blessed Nonnus gazed after her very intently for a long space of time. And after she had gone by, he turned round and still gazed after her. Then he turned towards the bishops sitting round him and said, 'Were you not delighted by such great beauty?' When they did not reply, he buried his face on his knees over the holy Bible which he held in his hands and all his emotion came out in tears; sighing deeply, he said again to the bishops, 'Were you not delighted by her great beauty?' Still they did not answer, so 'Indeed', he said, 'I was very greatly delighted and her beauty pleased me very much. See, God will place her before his awful and tremendous judgement seat and he will judge her on her gifts, just as he will judge us on our episcopal calling.' And he went on to say to the bishops, 'What do you think, beloved brothers, how many hours does this woman spend in her chamber giving all her mind and attention to adorning herself for the play, in order to lack nothing in beauty and adornment of the body; she wants to please all those who see her, lest those who are her lovers today find her ugly and do not come back tomorrow. Here are we, who have an almighty Father in heaven offering us heavenly gifts and rewards, our immortal Bridegroom, who promises good things to his watchmen, things that cannot be valued, 'which eye has not seen, nor ear heard, nor has it entered into the heart of man to know what things God has prepared for those who love him' (1 Cor.2.9). What else can I say? When we have such promises, when we are going to see the great and glorious face of our Bridegroom which has a beauty beyond compare, 'upon which the cherubim do not dare to gaze' (1 Pet.1.12), why do we not adorn ourselves and wash the dirt from our unhappy souls, why do we let ourselves lie so neglected?'

Cap. IV. When he had said all this, Bishop Nonnus took me, his sinful deacon, with him, and we went to the rooms we had been given for our lodging. Going into his bedchamber, the bishop threw himself on the ground with his face to the floor, and beating his breast he wept, saying, 'Lord Jesus Christ. I know I am a sinner and unworthy, for today the ornaments of a harlot have shone more brightly than the ornaments of my soul. How can I turn my face towards you? What words can justify me in your sight? I will not hide my heart from you, for you know all its secrets. Alas, I am a sinner and unworthy, for I stand before your altar and I do not offer you a soul adorned with the beauty you want to see in me. She promises to please men; I have promised to please you; and my filthiness makes me a liar. I am naked before earth and heaven, because I do not keep your commandments. I cannot put my hope in anything good that I do, but I place my trust in Your mercy which saves.' He said this kind of thing and wept for many hours; that day was a great festival of tears for us.

Cap. V. When day came, it was Sunday and after we had completed our night prayers, the holy bishop Nonnus said to me, 'I tell you, brother deacon, when I was asleep I was deeply disturbed and I do not understand it'. Then he told me the dream he had had: 'At the corner of the altar was a black dove, covered with soot, which flew around me and I could not bare the stench and filth of it. It stood by me until the prayer for the dismissal of the catechumens, and when the deacon announced to the catechumens, "Depart", no more was seen of it. After the prayer of the faithful, and the complete oblation had been offered and everyone had been dismissed, I came to the threshold of the house of God, and there

I saw the dove again, covered grievously with filth, and again it fluttered around me. Then I held out my hands and drew it to me, and plunged it into the font which was in the ante-chamber of the holy church and washed off all the dirt with which it was covered and it came out of the water as white as snow. It flew up into the highest heaven and was lost to my sight.' When the holy man of God, bishop Nonnus, had recounted his dream, he took me with him and brought me to the cathedral with the rest of the bishops and there we greeted the bishop of Antioch.

Cap. VI. He went in and preached to the people who came and sat around his throne and when he had read the canon of the holy Gospel, the same bishop of that city held the Gospel book towards the most blessed Nonnus and asked him to speak to the people. Nonnus then opened his mouth and spake by the wisdom of God, without any set speech or philosophy and with no indiscretion. Filled with the Holy Spirit, he exhorted and urged the people, speaking very earnestly about the future judgement and the good gifts in store in eternity. All the people were moved with compunction by his words, and the floor of the church was awash with the tears of the hearers.

Cap. VII. Now by the guiding hand of the mercy of God it happened that there came into the church that very harlot about whom I am speaking. What was even more marvellous was that she who was outside the church and had never before entered the house of God and had never before even considered her sins, was now suddenly pierced by the fear of the Lord when she heard bishop Nonnus preaching to the people. She was so struck that she despaired of herself and her tears flowed in such a flood that she could not control them. At once she gave orders to two of her servants: 'Stay in this place and when holy Nonnus the bishop comes out follow him, find out where he is lodging and come and tell me.' The servants did as their mistress ordered them, and followed us as far as the basilica of St Julianus which was near the place where we were lodging. They returned home and told their mistress, 'He is in the church of the most blessed Julianus'. When she heard this at once she sent the same servants for the *dyptiches* and on them she wrote: 'To the holy disciple of

Christ, greetings from a sinner and disciple of the devil. I have heard of your God, how he bent the heavens and came down to earth not for the righteous but for the salvation of sinners. So greatly did he humble himself that he came near to publicans, and he whom the cherubin do not dare to look upon (1 Pet.1.12) spoke with sinful men. My lord, you are very holy, and so, just as your lord Jesus shewed himself to the harlot in Samaria at the well (John 8.48) will you look upon me, as he did whose follower you are, as I have heard Christians say? If you are a true disciple of Christ, do not reject me, for through you I may deserve to see His face.' The holy bishop Nonnus wrote in reply, 'Whoever you are, show yourself to God and you will be saved. But I tell you, I am a man, a sinner, and a servant of God, and you would tempt my humanity. But if you really do desire God, have strength and faith and come to me among the other bishops, for I cannot let you see me alone.' When the harlot read this, filled with joy she came running to the church of the blessed martyr Julianus, and we were told that she was there. When Nonnus heard this, he called all the bishops around him, and ordered that she should be brought to him. When she came in where the bishops were gathered, she threw herself on the floor and seized the feet of the holy bishop Nonnus saying, 'I beg you, my lord, imitate your master the Lord Jesus Christ and pour out on me your goodness and make me a Christian. My lord, I am an ocean of sin, a deep pit of iniquity and I ask to be baptised.'

Cap. VIII. Bishop Nonnus could hardly persuade her to get up, but when she did, he said, 'The holy canons say that a harlot may not be baptised unless she has sponsors who will guarantee that she will not return to her old way of life.' When she heard this ruling of the bishops she threw herself on the floor again and seized the feet of Nonnus, washing them with her tears and wiping them with the hair of her head (Luke 7.38) saying, 'You will give account for my soul and to you I will confess all the sins I have committed: and you will wash away by baptism all my great sins and wickednesses. You will not now find a place with the saints before God unless you put away from me my evil deeds. Unless you give me rebirth as a bride of Christ and present me to God, you are no more than an apostate and idolater.' Then all the bishops and clergy which were there, when they saw how greatly this sinner desired God were amazed and said they had never before seen such faith and such desire for salvation as in this harlot: and at once they sent me, the sinful deacon, to the bishop of Antioch to tell him all about it and to ask him to send one of his deaconesses back with me. When he heard about it, he rejoiced with great joy saying, 'It is right, bishop Nonnus, that this great work should have waited for you. I know that you will speak for me in this matter.' At once he sent back with me the lady Romana, the first of the deaconesses. When we got back, we found the harlot still at the feet of the holy bishop Nonnus, who was with difficulty urging her to get up, saying, 'Get up, my daughter, so that I may exorcise you.' Then he said to her, 'Do you confess all your sins?' To which she replied, 'I have looked so closely into my heart that I cannot find there any single good action. I know my sins and they are more than the sand upon the sea-shore: water like the sea is little compared to the extent of my sins. But I trust in your God that he will forgive me the whole extent of my sinfulness and look upon me again.' Then the holy bishop Nonnus said, 'Tell me, what is your name?' and she replied, 'I was called Pelagia by my parents but the people of Antioch have called me Margaret (a pearl) because of the amount of jewelry with which my sins have adorned me; for I am decked out as a slave for the devil.' Nonnus said to her, 'Your natural name is Pelagia?' To which she replied, 'Yes, my lord.' Then Nonnus exorcised her and baptised her, placing on her the sign of the cross, and he gave her the Body of Christ. And with the lady Romana he was god-parent to her and the deaconess received her and took her to the place of the catechumens while we remained where we were. Then the bishop said to me, 'I tell you, brother deacon, today we are rejoicing with the angels of God, with the bread and wine of spiritual joy beyond measure, because of the salvation of this girl.'

Cap. IX. While we were eating some food, we suddenly heard sounds as of a man suffering violence and the devil cried out, saying, 'Alas, alas, what am I suffering from this decrepit old man? It was not enough for you to snatch from me three

thousand Saracens and baptise them, and obtain them for
your God. It was not enough for you that you took over Heli-
opolis and gave it to your God when it belonged to me and all
who lived there worshipped me. But now you have taken my
greatest hope from me and now more than ever I cannot bear
your schemes. Oh, how I suffer because of that accursed man!
Cursed be the day on which you were born! I am so weakened
that a river of tears flows from me, for my hope is taken
away.' The devil said all this outside, crying and lamenting,
and everyone heard him. When she returned, he said to the
newly-baptised girl, 'My lady Pelagia, why are you doing
this to me? Why have you become my Judas? For was not he
also crowned with glory and honour and became an apostate
by betraying his lord? This is what you have done to me!' The
holy Nonnus said to her, 'Make the sign of the Cross in the
name of Christ.' And she made the sign of the Cross in the
name of Christ and she blew at the demon and at once he disappeared.

Cap. X. Two days later, when Pelagia was asleep in her
room with the holy Romana her godmother, the devil
appeared to her in the night and awakened Pelagia the servant
of God, saying, 'I ask you, my lady Margaret, were you not
once rich with gold and silver? Did I not adorn you with gold
and jewels? Tell me, how have I displeased you? Tell me, so
that I may make amends, for you have made me a very great
cause for mockery among the Christians.' Then the handmaid Pelagia made the sign of the Cross and blew at the
demon, saying, 'My God who snatched me out of your teeth
and led me into the heavenly bridal chamber will resist you
for me.' At once the devil disappeared.

Cap. XI. On the third day after the baptism of the holy Pelagia, she called her servant who was in charge of all her goods
and said to him, 'Go to my rooms and make an inventory of
all the gold and silver, the ornaments and the precious
clothes, and bring it to me.' The servant did as his mistress
told him and reported it all to her. At once she sent for holy
Nonnus through the holy Romana her godmother, and she
placed all she had in his hands, saying, 'Lord, these are the
riches with which Satan ensnared me; I place them at your
disposal; do with them whatever you think is right, for my

choice is the riches of Christ.' At once the bishop called the senior custodian of the church and in her presence he gave all her goods into his hands saying, 'I charge you, by the undivided Trinity, do not let any of this remain with the bishop or with the church, but let it all be expended on the widows and orphans and the poor, so that whatever evil clings to it may be removed by this good use and the riches of sin become the treasures of righteousness. But if you sit lightly to this promise and either you or anyone else keep any of it, let anathema come upon you and them and their houses, and let them have a part with those who cry, 'Crucify, crucify.' Pelagia then called to all her servants, boys and girls, and set them free and gave each a collar of gold from her own hands and said, 'Make haste to free yourselves from this wicked world, so full of sin, so that we who have been together in this world may remain together without grief in that life which is most blessed.'

Cap. XII. On the eighth day when it is the custom for the baptised to take off their white robes, Pelagia rose in the night, though we did not know it, and took off her baptismal dress and put on a tunic and breeches belonging to the holy bishop Nonnus; and from that day she was never seen again in the city of Antioch. The holy lady Romana wept bitterly, but the holy bishop Nonnus said to her, 'Do not weep, my daughter, but rejoice with great joy, for Pelagia has chosen the better part (Luke 10.42) like Mary whom the Lord preferred to Martha in the Gospel.' Now Pelagia went to Jerusalem and built herself a cell on the mount of Olives and there she prayed to the Lord.

Cap. XIII. After a little while, the bishop of Antioch called the bishops together, so that they might all go back to their own homes. Three or four years later, I, James the deacon, wanted to go to Jerusalem to worship the resurrection of Christ and I asked the bishop to let me go. When he gave me his blessing he said to me, 'Brother deacon, when you reach the city of Jerusalem, ask the whereabouts of a certain brother Pelagius, a monk and a eunuch, who has lived there for some years shut up alone; go and visit him; truly I think you will be helped by him.' I did not at all understand that he was talking about the handmaid of God, Pelagia.

Cap. XIV. So I reached Jerusalem, and when I had joined in the adoration of the Resurrection of our Lord Jesus Christ, on another day I made inquiries about the servant of God. I went and found him on the mount of Olives where he used to pray to the Lord in a small cell which was closed on all sides, with one small window. I knocked on the window and at once she appeared and she recognised me, though I did not recognise her. How could I have known her again, with a face so emaciated by fasting? It seemed to me that her eyes had sunk inwards like a great pit. She said to me, 'Where have you come from, brother?' And I replied, 'I was sent to you by the order of the holy bishop Nonnus.' At once she closed the little window on me, saying, 'Tell him to pray for me, for he is a saint of God.' At once she began the psalms of the third hour. I prayed beside the cell and then left, much helped by the sight of her angelic face. I returned to Jerusalem and began to visit the brothers in the monasteries there.

Cap. XV. Throughout these monasteries, great indeed was the fame of the monk Pelagius. So I decided to make another journey to speak with her and receive some saving teaching. When I reached the cell and knocked, calling her name, there was no reply. I waited a second day and also a third, calling the name of Pelagius, but I could not hear anyone. Then I said to myself, 'Either there is no one there or he who was a monk has left.' But warned by a nudge from God, I said to myself, 'I had better see if, in fact, he has died.' So I broke open the little window; and I saw that he was dead. So I closed the opening and I was filled with sorrow. I ran all the way to Jerusalem and told whoever I met that the holy monk Pelagius who had wrought so many wonders was now at rest. Then the holy fathers came with monks from several monasteries and the door of the cell was broken in. They carried out his sacred little body as if it had been gold and silver they were carrying. When the fathers began to anoint the body with myrrh, they realised that it was a woman. They wanted to keep such a wonder hidden but they could not, because of the crowds of people thronging around, who cried out with a loud voice, 'Glory to you, Lord Jesus Christ, for you have hidden away on earth such great treasures, women as well as men.' So it was known to all the people, and monks came in from all the monasteries and also nuns, from Jericho and from the Jordan where the Lord was baptised, bearing candles and lamps and singing hymns; and the holy fathers bore her body to its burial.

May the life of this harlot, this account of total conversion, join us to her and bring us all to the mercy of the Lord on the day of judgement, to whom be glory and power and honour to the ages of ages. Amen.

CHAPTER FIVE

Thaïs; How to Receive a Gift

*Thaïs: 'For this let the choirs of heaven praise Him, and
all the little twigs and fresh green leaves on earth, all animals and the great waters. He is patient with us when we
fall; He is generous in His gifts when we repent.'*
*Paphnutius: 'He loves to be merciful; from all eternity
He has preferred pardon to punishment.'*[1]

The fourth prostitute whose story forms part of the collection
of literature about repentance was called Thaïs, and, like Pelagia, she plied her trade in one of the cities of Egypt; probably
Alexandria. Her name was the same as that of a famous courtesan who was said to have captivated Alexander the Great and
then his general Ptolomy First, by whom she had three children. She was also said to have provoked Alexander to set fire
to the Hundred Column Hall in Persepolis; her later namesake was also connected with fire (p. 83). In the story of Thaïs
the Harlot, as it was told among the monks of Egypt, she was
a prostitute, wealthy and beautiful, and so popular that her
many lovers even came to blows for her favour. Paphnutius,
one of the most famous names among the fathers of Egypt[2],
heard of the scandal. He disguised himself in secular clothing
and went to visit her. He spoke to Thaïs and she was struck to
the heart by his words, especially when he warned her about
the future judgement of God when she would be called to
account for all those she was causing to sin. Thaïs burned all
her goods and followed Paphnutius into the desert, where he
left her with a convent of nuns, immured in a cell with no
outlet, telling her to say only one prayer: 'You who made me,
have mercy upon me'. Three years later, Paphnutius went to
Scetis to talk to St Antony and his disciples about her, and
Paul, a disciple of Antony saw in a dream a rich bed in

heaven, prepared to receive Thaïs into glory. Paphnutius realised that this indicated her forgiveness and went to her cell. He insisted that she come out, even though she now wanted to stay there; fifteen days later she was dead.

It is a harsh, uncompromising tale, with none of the literary flourishes or humane touches that make the other stories attractive. But in some ways, just because of its brevity, the fundamental pattern of the story emerges more clearly. It was a popular tale in the desert and there are other accounts of similar incidents, of which the story of Maria, niece of Abraham, is one (pp. 92–101). Another is told in the *Sayings of the Desert Fathers* about John the Dwarf, and the woman Paësia:

The parents of a young girl died and she was left an orphan; she was called Paësia. She decided to make her house a hospice for the use of the fathers of Scetis. But in course of time her resources were exhausted and she began to be in want. Some wicked men came to see her and turned her aside from her aim. She began to live an evil life to the point of becoming a prostitute. The fathers, learning this, were deeply grieved and they called John the Dwarf and said to him, 'We have learned that this sister is living an evil life. While she could she gave us charity, so now it is our turn to offer her charity and to go to her assistance. Go to see her then and according to the wisdom that God has given you, put things right for her'. So abba John went to see her and said to the old doorkeeper, 'Tell your mistress I am here'. But she sent him away saying, 'From the start you ate her goods and see how poor she is now'. Abba John said, 'Tell her I have something that will be very helpful to her'. The doorkeeper's children mocked him saying, 'What have you to give her that you want to meet her?' He replied, 'How do you know what I am going to give her?' The old woman went up and spoke to her mistress about him. Paësia said to her, 'Those monks are always going about around the Red Sea and finding pearls.' Then she got ready and said to the doorkeeper, 'Please bring him to me'. As he was coming up, she got ready for him and lay down on the bed. Abba John entered and sat beside her. Looking into her eyes, he said, 'What

have you got against Jesus that you behave like this?'
When she heard this she became completely rigid. Then
abba John bent his head and began to weep copiously.
She asked him, 'Why are you crying, father?' He raised
his head, then lowered it again weeping and said to her,
'I see Satan playing in your face, how should I not
weep?' Hearing this she said, 'Father, is it possible to
repent?' He replied, 'Yes'. She said, 'Take me wherever
you wish.' 'Let us go', he said and she got up and went
with him. Abba John noticed that she did not make any
arrangements about her house; he said nothing but he
was surprised. When they reached the desert the evening
was drawing on. He made a little pillow in the sand and
marked it with the cross, saying, 'Sleep here'. Then he
did the same for himself a little further on, said his
prayers and lay down. Waking in the middle of the
night, he saw a shining path reaching from heaven to her
and he saw the angels of God bearing away her soul.
When he saw that she was dead, he threw himself down-
ward on the ground praying to God and he heard this:
'One single hour of repentance has brought her more
than the penances of many who continue without show-
ing such fervour in repentance.'[3]

Paësia was someone known to the monks and their care for
her was in response to her charity towards them. She is
another instance of a well-to-do woman who used her wealth
freely and lavishly for the benefit of the ascetics. John the
Dwarf was held to be like Paphnutius, one of the strongest of
the desert fathers and therefore both able to walk into a com-
promising situation with safety and one who would also have
the desire to take such a risk for love of another person.

Another story of this type is told about an anonymous
monk, said to be very experienced in the ascetic life, this time
in connection with his natural sister:

He had a promiscuous sister in the city who brought
many souls to ruin. The old men often pestered the
brother about her, and they were able to persuade him to
go to her and somehow, by warning her, to stop sin
from occurring because of her. As he arrived in that
place one of her friends saw him and went to tell her,
announcing, 'Your brother is at the door'. She, deeply

disturbed, left the customer she was serving and at the sight of her brother jumped up with her head uncovered. She attempted to embrace him but he said to her, 'My dear sister, save your own soul, for through you many have been lost. How will you endure sharp and eternal torture?' She began to tremble and said to him, 'Do you think that there is salvation for me after all this?' And he said to her, 'If you will it, there is salvation'. She cast herself at her brother's feet and begged him to take her with him into the desert. He said to her, 'Put your cloak over your head and follow me'. She said to him, 'Let us go now, for it is better for me to have my head un-covered and be unseemly than to enter the workshop of wickedness'. As they made their way, he urged her to repent. They saw some people coming to meet them and he said to her, 'Since not everyone knows that you are my sister, go off a little way from the road until they have passed by'. After a while, he called to her, 'Let us go on our way, sister'. When she did not answer him, he turned and found her dead. He saw that her footprints were bloody for she had been barefoot.[4]

Another version of the story which is very close to the story of Thaïs was told about Abba Serapion, though in this case the enclosure in a cell was gradual, and at the request of the prostitute herself. After persuading the prostitute to follow him to the desert, the story continues:

The old man took her to a monastery of virgins and entrusted her to the amma and said, 'Take this sister and do not put any yoke or commandment on her as on the others sisters but if she wants something give it to her and allow her to walk where she wishes'. After some days the courtesan said, 'I am a sinner; I wish to eat every second day'. A little later she said, 'I have committed many sins; I wish to eat every fourth day'. A few days later she besought the amma saying, 'Since I have grieved God greatly by my sins, do me the kindness of putting me in a cell and shutting it completely and giving me a little bread and some work through the window'. The amma did so, and the woman pleased God for the rest of her life.[5]

In each instance, the story is stark and totally without sentimentality. Anatole France was appalled by the story of Thaïs, as his novel shows.[6] He modified the details of Thaïs' enclosure, even when the theme of his work (the misguidedness of the proud and passionate ascetic) would have benefited by the more unpleasant side of the story. The Paphnutius of his novel lacks any respect for humanity, and provides a classic instance of a plain, bullying fanatic. But to be sealed for years in a fetid cell went beyond the sensibility of a nineteenth century Frenchman. It is possible that the writer of the Thaïs story himself thought Paphnutius' action extreme, since he presents him as being worried about his penitent, and includes a vision of the salvation of Thaïs which secures her liberation from her penitential cell. Paphnutius had, in any case, a name in the desert for toughness and, if he can at all be identified with the sayings that went under his name, this was his chief characteristic.

These stories, if read as historical accounts of events, are not attractive; but if they are approached as stories about the essence of repentance constructed around the facts, certain valuable insights can be apprehended. In each case, the monk who undertakes the visit in disguise to a brothel is presented as a strong person, firm in his ascetic life, to whom no stain of scandal could be attached. Each speaks alone with the woman and at once, in a face to face dialogue, confronts her with the danger of her way of life, not only to herself but to others. There is no analysis or discussion or excuse; just the plain insistence on the presence of Christ here and now, and his call to the person there and then. This light of reality, the truth of the women's situation before God, is uncompromising, and in each case strikes at the heart and touches the core of reality in each of the women involved. Unable to trust their own ideas and reactions, they take the sensible course of placing themselves in the hands of those who have revealed this truth to them, and at once each follows the opportunity for freedom that is so unexpectedly offered. In the case of Paësia and the sister of the monk, they enter at once into the kingdom of heaven; there is no need for a longer repentance, their return to God is made definitive by their death in which they receive the gift of free salvation totally. In the story of Thaïs, a different point is made: Thaïs is sealed into a cell as if into a tomb, a limitation down to one point of reality before God; and this is enforced by her one prayer, 'You who made me, have mercy upon me'. Creature before creator, sinner before saviour, she is shown as experiencing the escape from illusion, untruth, self-determination, hardness and the inability to love or be loved, alone and in darkness, through three years. A shock-treatment, perhaps, but not imposed by alien cruelty; it was asked for and given out of love. There is no analysis of her sins: she is simply before God; and in the end Paphnutius claims that she has received full forgiveness, not because of any penances but simply because she remained in this light of truth before God. As with Mary of Egypt, there is no question of working to earn forgiveness by penances or self-analysis; the forgiveness of God is a free gift, salvation is freely given. All Thaïs, Paësia and the sister of the monk can do is learn how to receive the gift in reality and in their whole lives. Any hardness is a result of that moment, not a cause. Moreover, Thaïs, and this is true of all these women, needs another person at this moment of turning towards God. This fact expresses an important truth: repentance is not done alone but within the Church, even for Mary of Egypt: she in some respects was totally alone, yet at the end of her life she needed both Zossima and the sacraments.

However harsh the story of Thaïs sounds, nevertheless it was used as the basis for a medieval play of particular elegance and vigour. Hrotswitha, a canoness of the royal abbey of Gandersheim in the tenth century, wrote plays in the manner of Terence but with the theme of christian chastity as their subject. That one should be based on the story of Maria, the niece of Abraham, is not surprising, since it is a tale full of human sympathy, but her choice of the story of Thaïs for her second play on the theme of the redemption of a prostitute is less obvious.[7] In the play, Paphnutius retains the harshness Hrotswitha found in the early accounts of him, and Thaïs matches his abrasive manner; their drama is one of dynamic love and vivid repentance. The words Paphnutius uses when he goes to visit Thaïs are from the Song of Songs: 'Arise, my love, my beautiful one, and come away' (Song of Songs 1.1). The central scene of the play is a scene passed over in the older account: it is a vivid re-enactment of the burning of all her goods by Thaïs in public. There is an urgency and vigour about the play which brings to life the story and makes the moment of the enclosure of the delicate and luxury-loving girl in a cell, dark and small and without outlet even for her own filth, one of dramatic tension and human credibility. The death of Thais ends the play, as she dies with Paphnutius beside her and the same prayer which she used in her cell, now by choice the only words on her lips: 'You who made me, have pity upon me'.[8] A contrast is continually drawn in Hrotswitha's play between earthly beauty and the true beauty of the spirit, which is attained by the refusal of Thaïs to be held by the attractions of the body which she has previously enjoyed. The play illustrates the theme of the story: 'Grace is the free gift of God and does not depend on our merits'[9], and in order to do this, Hrotswitha adds a dimension of human emotion and sensitivity that is lacking in the stark versions of the earlier texts: in doing so, she in no way diminishes, but rather enhances the truth to be conveyed.

NOTES TO CHAPTER FIVE

The text of the *Life of St Thaïs, the Harlot* is found in PL 73, cols. 661–62; Acta SS, Oct. IV, 224. (*BHL* 8012).

1. Hrotswitha of Gandesheim, *Comoedia*, 'Paphnutius', PL 137, cols. 1027–46. English trans. Christopher St John, *The Plays of Hrotswitha* (London, 1912). (*BHL* 8018).
2. For sayings of Paphnutius, *Sayings*. Also *Lives of the Desert Fathers*, 14.
3. *Sayings*, John the Dwarf 40.
4. *World*, pp. 23–24.
5. *Sayings*, Serapion 1.
6. Anatole France, *Thaïs* (Paris, 1902).
7. Hrotswitha, '*Paphnutius*', PL 137, cols. 1027–1046.
8. *Ibid*. col. 1046.
9. *Ibid*. col. 1045.

English translation of the *Life of St Thaïs the Harlot* from a Latin translation of a Greek text by an anonymous author.

Cap. I. There was a certain harlot called Thaïs and she was so beautiful that many for her sake sold all that they had and reduced themselves to utter poverty; quarrels arose among her lovers and often the doorstep of this girl's house was soaked in the blood of young men. When Abba Paphnutius heard about it, he put on secular clothes and went to see her in a certain city in Egypt. He handed her a silver piece as the price for committing sin. She accepted the price and said, 'Let us go inside'. When he went in, he sat down on the bed which was draped with precious covers and he invited her, saying, 'If there is a more private chamber, let us go in there.' She said, 'There is one, but if it is people you are afraid of, no one ever enters this room; except, of course, for God, for there is no place that is hidden from the eyes of divinity.' When the old man heard this, he said to her, 'So you know there is a God?' She answered him, 'I know about God and about the eternal kingdom and also about the future torments of sinners'. 'But if you know this,' he said, 'why are you causing the loss of so many souls so that you will be condemned to render an account not only of your own sins but of theirs as well?' When Thaïs heard this, she threw herself at the feet of Paphnutius and begged him with tears, 'Give me a penance, Father, for I trust to find forgiveness by your prayers. I beg you to wait for just three hours, and after that, wherever you tell me to go, I will go, and whatever you tell me to do, I will do it.' So Paphnutius arranged a meeting place with her and she went out and collected together all the goods that she had received by her sins and piled them all together in the middle of the city, while all the people watched, saying, 'Come here, all of you who have sinned with me, and see how I am burning whatever you gave me'. The value of it was forty pounds.

Cap. II. When it was all consumed, she went to the place that the father had arranged with her. Then he sought out a monastery of virgins and took her into a small cell, sealing the door with lead and leaving only a small opening through which food could be passed to her and he ordered her to be given daily a little bread and a little water by the sisters of the monastery. When Thaïs realised that the door was sealed with lead, she said to him, 'Father, where do you want me to urinate?' and he replied, 'In the cell, as you deserve.' Then she asked him how she should pray to God, and he said to her, 'You are not worthy to name God, or to take his divine name upon your lips, or to lift up your hands to heaven, for your lips are full of sin and your hands are stained with iniquity; only stand facing towards the east and repeat often only this: "You who made me, have mercy upon me".'

Cap. III. When she had been enclosed in this way for three years, Paphnutius began to be anxious, and so he went to see abba Antony, to ask him if her sins had been forgiven by the Lord or not. When he arrived, he recounted the affair to him in detail, and Abba Antony called together all his disciples and they agreed to keep vigil all night and each of them to persist in prayer so that God might reveal to one of them the truth of the matter about which Paphnutius had come. Each retired to his cell and took up continuous prayer. Then Paul, the great disciple of St Antony, suddenly saw in the sky a bed adorned with precious cloths and guarded by three virgins whose faces shone with brightness. Then Paul said to them; 'Surely so great a glory can only be for my father Antony?' but a voice spoke to him saying, 'This is not for your father Antony, but for the harlot Thaïs.' Paul went quickly and reported what he had heard and seen and Paphnutius recognised the will of God and set off for the monastery where the girl was enclosed. He began to open the door for her which he had sealed up, but she begged to be left shut up in there. When the door was open he said to her, 'Come out, for God has forgiven you your sins.' She replied, 'I call God to witness that since I came in here my sins have always been before my eyes as a burden; they have never been out of my sight and I have always wept to see them.' Abba Paphnutius said to her, 'God has forgiven your sins not because of your penances but because you have always had the remembrance of your sins in your soul.' When he had taken Thaïs out, she lived for fifteen days and then passed away in peace.

CHAPTER SIX

Maria the Niece of Abraham; an Image of Salvation

In the deserts of the heart
Let the healing fountain start:
In the prison of his days
Teach the free man how to praise[1]

Each of the stories considered so far have been about women who pursued a dissolute life in the world and turned to the new life in the desert. The final story in the group is rather different. It is about a flight from the desert to the brothel and a return. This is the last story told by Ephraim the Deacon in his account of the life of Abraham, a monk whom he revered and loved. It tells how Abraham brought up his orphaned niece, the child Maria, from the age of seven, and how she was seduced by a visiting monk; how she fled in despair to the city and lived as a prostitute until her uncle found her and persuaded her to return with him to the desert where she lived a life of repentance until her death.

There are many points of great interest about this story, both in its content and in its form. First, who wrote it and for what audience? The author is 'Ephraim the Deacon'. Like James, he was a deacon (in fact, an archdeacon),[2] as well as a monk; he was therefore among the literate. He was a disciple of Abraham, and he wrote an account of the life of his master for the edification of his brother monks: 'Lo, I, a mediocre person and unlearned, even I talked with this perfect and best of men'.[3] He tells the stories about Abraham as a modern instance of a life totally filled with God, even though, as he says, the colours of the picture are at times dark and sad. Abraham and Ephraim are mentioned also by Sozoman,[4] and there was an Abba Abraham to whom certain sayings of the fathers were attributed[5], who may be the same man.

85

When Hrotswitha of Gandersheim wrote a play on the theme of this story of Maria,[6] she brought the figure of Ephraim forward from the relatively obscure part he gives himself in his own account and makes explicit his role as confidant and friend of Abraham in some moving dialogue. At the end of his own account there is a coda[7] which is more self-revealing than the accounts written from the viewpoint of Zossima, or by the deacon James; no doubt it was that which moved Hrotswitha to expand his part in her play. In this epilogue, Ephraim writes as an old man following the death of his friends and heroes, Abraham and Maria: the 'stars' of the ascetic life have gone out, leaving him alone in old age on the threshold of death. Limited now by age and weakness, he sees his life as a failure in which the golden moments of glory were reflected for him through the other two; they have gone and 'the long quiet of winter finds me alone and unready'. One of those who observe and write, he knows he was not one of those that do; only the prayers of his friends the saints – the stars – can give him hope; and in this he is surely alongside his readers. Whether Ephraim is reporting what he has seen, or whether he is making a more complex work out of several incidents with which he was familiar, his art as a story-teller is undoubted. He appears discreetly in his own narrative, giving the reader a point of observation towards the central characters, and, at the end, he concludes the story by writing his own reactions to it.

Secondly, there is much of interest here in forming a picture of life in the desert, by comparing the text with details from other sources. The presence of children among the ascetics was not, for instance, unknown. In the *Sayings of the Desert Fathers* there is a story of Carion who became a monk in Scetis and took with him his small son, Zacharias, to share his cell and his monastic life.[8] In Cassian's *Institutes*, there is a story of Patermucius, who was received as a monk together with his son who was eight years old;[9] the younger Paula was dedicated to monastic life from infancy and was in a convent in Bethlehem before she was sixteen;[10] in the *Life of Mary of Egypt*, Zossima was said to have been a monk from his infancy (p. 36). This custom was not without dangers, and later in Scetis a monk said, 'Do not bring young boys here;

four churches in Scetis have been destroyed because of boys'.[11] This story is unusual in presenting a hermit as educating a girl. They live in twin cells and say their offices together. Another side of life in the desert is demonstrated by their distrust of material goods. Abraham and Maria both regarded material possessions as impediments to the freedom of life in the desert, first, when Abraham treated the child Maria as a disciple by giving her inheritance away to the poor to prevent distraction and the responsibilities of the life of the world, and later, when Maria herself simply left all her wealth to return to the desert; like Pelagia, who gave away her goods, and Thaïs, who burned them. This is a fundamental part of the desert tradition in which material goods are the first bond with the world which has to be decisively cut in order to attain the freedom of heart. Another detail from this tale of some interest in forming a picture of the world of the desert fathers, is the fact that the dress of a soldier is seen as a fitting disguise for Abraham when visiting a brothel; this is no doubt a reflection of the conscripts for the Roman army in Egypt. The gold piece offered to the brothel-keeper is a reminder of the gold of Egypt, that rich province of the Empire. The brothel-keeper and the elegant, leisurely meal ordered before the main events of the evening also offer a glimpse into the society of a city in the ancient world.

Thirdly, there are here two spiritual themes found frequently in other desert material which are of major importance: the first is the monk who sins: and the second is the good man who adopts a disguise in order to visit a brothel to deliver an inmate. To take the fallen monk theme first: the desert literature is not concerned with stories of the automatically pious, but with the repentance of sinners, and among such stories there are examples of monks who failed, either temporarily or permanently. What is 'failure' in the desert? It is not simply sexual, genital experience, though that is by definition renounced completely in the monastic life. Sexual intercourse, indeed, contradicts the very essence of the life undertaken, but for this as for all sins there is forgiveness. What really lies outside the ascetic life is not lust itself but despair, the proud attitude which denies the possibility of forgiveness. Like the fallen monk in John of Lycopolis' story,[12]

Maria had done everything right all her life but without learning the essential lesson of the desert; utter dependence on God
alone for mercy. So overcome by a passion stronger than her
delicate self-control, she sinned with the 'monk by name
only' (p. 93) and at once despaired of forgiveness. She could
not bear to tell Abraham and Ephraim what had happened;
instead, she fled by night and continued in the acts which had
caught her. As Abraham saw so aptly in a dream, she was like
a bird drawn into a serpent's mouth. In the moving conver-
sation between the old hermit and Maria in the brothel, he has
no word of condemnation for her but speaks only about
mercy and love: 'Why did you not tell us? Would not Ephraim and I have shared your penance? . . . Have I not come to
bring you home, my child?' (p. 98). There is no discussion of
motive or responsibility for the past, and faced with her
uncle's compassionate love Maria's heart is touched; weeping, she says, 'because you have so grieved for me, even
coming down into this pit of filth; therefore she repents' (p.
99). It is not judgement or discussion of sins, excuses, or understanding of alleviating circumstances that break the heart,
but mercy and love. This is a fundamental aspect of the life of
the desert fathers: not to judge but to love:

> They said of Abba Macarius the Great that he became, as
> it is written, a god upon earth, because just as God pro-
> tects the world, so Abba Macarius would cover the
> faults that he saw as though he did not see them, and
> those which he heard as though he did not hear them.[13]

The second theme, that of the monk disguised, has already
been discussed in the analysis of the story of Thaïs, but here
the idea, as it is expressed in Ephraim's subtle account, provides a vital key to the whole literature we are considering.
When Ephraim has described how Abraham put on an alien
dress to go and seek his niece in the city, he refers to a minor
and, at first sight, inappropriate incident in the life of his
namesake, the patriarch Abraham:

> Let us marvel, brothers, at this second Abraham, for as
> the first Abraham went out to battle against the kings
> and delivered his nephew Lot, so this second Abraham
> went to war with the devil that he might overcome him

and bring back his niece Maria with even greater triumph (p. 95).

The reference is to Genesis 14.14–16, and the rescue of Lot
by his uncle Abraham from the 'four kings with five' who
had captured him:

> When Abraham heard it, to wit, that his brother Lot was
> taken he numbered of the servants born in his house
> three hundred and eighteen well appointed; and persued
> them to Dan ... and he brought back all the substance
> and his brother Lot with his substance, the women also
> and the people.

The obvious links between the two stories are grammatical
ones: the same name, Abraham, and the same word, *nepos*
(niece or nephew), to express the relationship between both
Abraham and Lot and Abraham and Maria. Given this link,
the mind of any reader in the ancient or medieval world
would be quick to see the hidden meaning Ephraim is presenting. In early commentaries on this text from Genesis, or
any other text, it is not the literal or historical meaning that
interested the reader; as Origen said:

> If anyone wants to hear or understand (this) according to
> the literal sense, he ought to listen with the Jews rather
> than with the Christians. But if he wants to be a Chris-
> tian and a disciple of Paul, let him hear what is said
> according to the 'law of the Spirit' and let him consider
> what is said about Abraham and his wife and sons allego-
> rical. We are given such allegories, but it is not easy for
> anyone to discover all their meaning, so we must pray
> from our hearts that 'the veil might be taken away'. If
> anyone wants to be converted to the Lord, 'for the Lord
> is the Spirit', let him pray from his heart that the veil of
> the letter might be taken away and the light of the Spirit
> come, as it is said, 'we all behold with open face as in a
> glass the glory of the Lord and are changed into that
> image from glory to glory even as by the Lord the
> Spirit'.[14]

The literal sense of a text was far too thin to hold the interest of a reader in the ancient world; the surface meaning of
any work, in the classical as well as the christian world, was a

doorway through which the reader could pass into many and varied worlds. It was not only more interesting, it was more useful for the work of salvation to seek for hidden meanings of a text beneath the surface of the letters: 'Blessed are the eyes' wrote Claudius of Turin in his preface to a commentary on the scriptures, 'that see Divine Spirit through the letter's veil'.[15] For the monks, this way of reading and understanding scripture was essential and very practical:

> they took care never to let one word escape them without their knowing the meaning thereof not as a mere matter of history . . . but spiritually, according to the interpretation of the Fathers, that is to say, they applied all the psalms to their own lives and works and to their passions and to their spiritual life and to the wars which the devils waged against them.[16]

Readers accustomed to this way of looking at the text of the Bible readily applied it also to other texts, and often the spiritual interpretation of a scriptural passage briefly alluded to in a sermon would be so well known that this knowledge would automatically illuminate the later text. This story of Maria and Abraham is a case in point. The Fathers saw in Abraham's leaving of his own place to save a captive, the image of Christ himself: 'Here we see', wrote Bede, 'Abraham as the mystical figure of Christ, who by His passion and death redeemed the world from death in battle against the devil'.[17] Commentaries on an earlier verse in this chapter of Genesis had established that Lot was an image of the human soul: the 'four kings against five' (Gen. 14.9) were seen as the four elements and the five senses. Lot, carried captive by the four kings with five, became then a figure of the human soul carried off, captive, by the passions. Maria, like Lot, had been taken prisoner by sensuality, and in the same way mankind had been gripped by sin. Both Abrahams were therefore the Christ, the deliverer from sin: 'He went forth to do battle with the cross of Christ and in the name of Jesus that strong sign, that banner of faith'.[18] The monk Abraham, moreover, hid his true nature in order to enter into a place of sin for the sake of saving a sinner; even so, Christ emptied himself so as not to be recognised by the Devil, in order to save his prey from hell. In this way, the stories of the Old Testament and the realities of the New, are focused by the contemporary story for the sake of the hearers. It is a good reminder that these stories are not newspaper accounts or biographies, concerned with the psychological reactions and relationships of the protagonists; if they were they would be woefully inadequate. They are rather theologies, and they relate not to past events but to the present situation of the one who hears or reads. These stories were written to answer the question in the mind of the reader, 'Why am I told this?', not the question, 'How did this come about?' They are deliberately told to demand the response of the reader, not to present historical facts as such. They are not best described as fiction, but rather as part of the long tradition of christian hagiography, in which the events recounted are related to the person of Christ the redeemer, for the benefit of the reader or hearer.

NOTES TO CHAPTER SIX

The text of the *Life of Maria the Niece of Abraham, Vita Sanctae Mariae, Meretricis* is found in PL 73, cols. 651–60. (*BHL* 12). There is an English translation by Helen Waddell, *The Desert Fathers*, pp. 283–303.

1. W. H. Auden, 'In Commemoration of W. B. Yeats', *Collected Shorter Poems, 1927–1957* (London, 1966), p. 143.
2. Ephraim the Deacon is not to be confused with Ephraim the Syrian.
3. *Life of St Abraham*, PL 73, cols. 281–94; the story of Maria is printed later in the volume but is in fact the conclusion of the *Life of St Abraham*.
4. Sozomen, *Ecclesiastical History* III,15.
5. *Sayings*, Abraham 1–4.
6. Hrotswitha, *Abraham*, PL 137, cols. 1013–28; translated by Christopher St John, *The Plays of Hrotswitha* (London, 1923), pp. 71–89. (*BHL* 13.)
7. cf. PL 73, col. 660, which suggests that though these passages are lacking in the MS from which the text is printed, they are found elsewhere and belong here.
8 *Sayings*, Carion 2.
9. John Cassian, *Institutions Cenobitique*, text and translation by J. C. Guy (Paris, 1965), Bk. IV, 27.

10. Jerome, Letter 134.
11. *Sayings*, Isaac of the Cells 5.
12. *Lives*, John of Lycopolis 32.
13. *Sayings*, Macarius 32.
14. Origen, *Homilia in Genesim* 6:1, ed. Doutreleau, SC 7 (Paris, 1976).
15. Claudius of Turin, *In Libros Informationum Litterae et Spiritus super Leviticum Praefatio*, PL 104, col. 615.
16. *The Paradise of the Fathers*, translated by Wallace A. Budge (London, 1934), 'Questions and Answers on the Ascetic Rule' no. 637, vol. 2, pp. 306–7.
17. Bede,*Commentarii in Lib. Genesis*, cap. xiv, ed. J. A. Giles (London 1843), pp. 173–4.
18. *ibid.*

English translation of the *Life of Maria the Harlot*, niece of Abraham the Hermit, written by the Archdeacon Ephraim; translated into Latin by an anonymous translator.

Cap. I. Now, dearly beloved, I want to tell you about something the blessed man (Abraham) did in his old age, an affair which ought to provoke wonder in each one of you. To wise and spiritual men it is full of edification, an example not lacking in humility and compassion. This heroic deed happened like this:

Cap. II. The blessed man Abraham had a natural brother who lived close by, and he died, leaving a daughter aged seven. When friends of her father realised that she was left without parents, they brought her to her uncle. When the old man understood the situation, he arranged for her to be placed in a room built on to the outside wall of his hermitage. Now, there was a window in between the two cells, one on either side, through which he taught her the Psalter and the other Scriptures; she kept vigil there with him, singing the praises of the Lord; she sang psalms without number and strove to emulate her uncle in all his ascetic practices. Very soon she had learned the principles, and was proficient in them; at once she made use of every virtue in her soul. The holy man prayed for her all the time to the Lord with tears, so that her mind might not be entangled in the affairs of this world, for when he died her father had left her untold riches. At the death of his brother, and when the daughter had fled to him, at once the servant of Christ had ordered it all to be given away to the needy and the orphans. It was her uncle's daily prayer that she might be kept safe from the snares of the Devil and the traps of wicked thoughts. So she held constantly to the rules he taught her. Her uncle was glad to see how she at once made progress without any hesitation in all the virtues, that is to say, in tears, humility, modesty, and quietness, and in that virtue which is best because it is the one chosen by God, charity. So she passed twenty years with him in ascetic life, living like an unspotted lamb or untouched dove, and when that space of time was over, the Devil became enraged against her and he laid out his usual snares to catch her in his nets, so that in some way he might strike out also at the goodness and care of the blessed old man and in some small way take his attention away from the Lord.

Cap. III. Now there was a certain man, a monk by name only, who often used to come to visit him, under the pretext of seeking edification. He could not see the blessed girl at all because of the window, but he was filled with the urgings of lust and he used to try to speak with her, love, or rather lust burning in his heart like fire. He lay in ambush for her for a long time, and for the full circle of a year he softened her thoughts by his words. Then one day he came to her cell window and she climbed down to him; at once he defiled and polluted her by intercourse out of wicked iniquity and lust. Afterwards, she was appalled in her heart at the magnitude of the sin she had committed, and when she had put on her clothes again she beat her face with her hands, wishing, in such great grief, that she were dead. She was swayed by thoughts of diverse passions and so overcome with anxiety that she could see no way out of the situation. She lamented that she was not what she had been and cried out, 'I feel as if I am dead already; I have lost all that I had before by the hard work of asceticism; all my prayers, tears and vigils have come to nothing. I have angered God and destroyed myself. Alas, I am utterly miserable. I ought to become a fountain all made of tears. I have brought down sorrow upon my most holy uncle. The shame, o my soul, overwhelms me. I have been mocked by the devil. What is there for me but wretchedness if I live any longer? Alas for me, what have I done, what have I made myself? Alas, alas, what evil have I done, in what manner have I failed! How is my mind darkened! I did not understand what it would be like to fall, nor how I would be contaminated. I did not know what clouds of darkness would cover my heart. How can I ever forget what I have done? Whither shall I flee, where shall I go, in what cesspit shall I throw myself? Oh, where is now all the teaching of my most holy uncle? What has become of the counsel of his friend, Ephraim? They taught me to endure as a virgin, urging me to keep my soul unspotted for the eternal Bridegroom, for, they said, your Spouse is holy and He is jealous. Alas for me, what have I done, for I dare not look up to heaven since I know myself to be dead, before God and men. I will never again dare to come to that window, for how can I, a sinner, covered with filth, ever speak again to my uncle? If I were to dare to do so, fire would come out of that window and consume me. It is better for me to go right away to another country where there is nothing that would remind me of all this, to which I am now dead; there is now no hope of salvation for me.' So she got up and fled away to another city, changed her appearance and began to ply her trade in a brothel.

Cap. IV. While the ruin of the aforesaid woman was taking place, the blessed man was warned of it in a dream. For he saw a huge and terrible snake of foul appearance come out hissing and it went towards her cell. There he saw it snatch a dove and swallow her, crushing her in its jaws. Abraham was stirred and grieved and he wept bitterly, for he thought it meant that a persecution was to be stirred up by Satan against the Church and that many would turn against the faith, or that some kind of schism would beset the Church. So he knelt down and prayed to the Lord, saying, 'You know all things, you love mankind, show me what is hidden in this dream'. Two days later he saw the snake come into his own cell, and place its head under his feet and die; an lo, the dove it had devoured was alive in its stomach and Abraham reached out and took her out alive. Astonished, he called again and again to the blessed girl, thinking she was in her cell and he said, 'What has vexed you, my daughter Maria, (for this was his name for her) for two days now you have not opened your mouth in the praises of God?' But there was no reply nor did he hear her reading the psalms as usual, and so he realised that his dream must have been about her. Then he groaned and wept bitterly, and weeping he said, 'Alas, a most cruel wolf has snatched my lamb away; my daughter has been taken away as a prisoner.' Then raising his voice he cried with tears, 'Christ, Saviour of the world, give me back my lamb, Maria, and restore her to the flock alive, that I may not in my old age go out of this world in sorrow. Lord, do not despise my prayer but send your grace at once and snatch her unhurt from the mouth of the snake.' Then for the two days that has passed in his dream, two years passed by, in which the life of his child went on as if in the stomach of a most foul snake. And all the time the holy man prayed constantly day and night for her to the Lord.

Cap. V. Now after two years, in order to learn where she was and how she was living, he called for someone very well known to him and asked him to make inquiries. Then this man found her, and with great pity for him in his heart, he brought back the news. At once the old man asked him to get him a horse and the dress of a soldier, so that he might go and find her without being recognised. So Abraham put on the dress of a soldier and put a large hat on his head so that it hid his face, and he opened the door of his cell. He took with him a pound's weight in coins, and getting on the horse he hastened away. He went through the countryside to the city, adopting the customs of the inhabitants so that he might not be recognised. Thus blessed Abraham made use of an alien dress that he might turn her back from her flight. Let us marvel, brethren, at this second Abraham, for as the first Abraham went into battle with the kings and brought out his nephew, Lot, so this second Abraham went to war with the Devil so that he might overcome him, and bring back his niece with even more triumph.

Cap. VI. Now when he reached the place, he went into the brothel, and he looked all round very carefully to see if he could find the one he was seeking. When he had done this for

some time, he wanted to arrange to see her with the least possible interruption, so he went up to the brothel-keeper and
smiled, saying, 'My friend, I hear that you have a very good
girl indeed here; if I may, I would very much like to have her'.
The brothel-keeper saw that he had grey hair and judged him
to be very old, and in order therefore to encourage the stir-
rings of lust in such a one, she said, 'As you say, I have one
who is beautiful beyond the usual run; her beauty excels
everything that nature can create'. The old man then asked
her name, and she replied that she was called Maria. Smiling
with joy, Abraham then said, 'I beg you to take me into her
presence, so that I may enjoy her today, for I have heard this
girl praised by many'. When the brothel-keeper heard this,
she summoned Maria, and when her uncle saw her in the
dress of an harlot he was almost overcome by grief and the
sadness of his soul almost drove the smile from his face; he
had to hold back his tears by force, lest the brothel-keeper
should know him and make him leave the courtyard.

Cap. VII. When they had rested and drunk a little, this
amazing man began to fondle her; he got up and put his arms
around her neck and stroked it with his lips. When his lips
touched her, Maria smelt the sweet smell of asceticism
coming from his body and she remembered the days when
she, too, had lived as an ascetic; and as if pierced by a spear she
cried out from her heart and burst into tears, unable to bear it;
and she said as if to herself, 'Alas, alas, how desolate I am!'
The brothel-keeper was angry when she noticed this, and said
in surprise, 'Whatever is the matter with you, Mistress
Maria, that you should suddenly start crying like this? You
have been here for two years and never before have I had a
word or groan of complaint from you. I do not know what
has come over you now.' Maria said to her, 'It were better for
me if I could die before the third year has passed.' At this, the
blessed old man was afraid she would recognise him, so he
said soothingly to her, 'If you go on thinking about your sins,
how can we expect to enjoy ourselves?' Oh most high God,
how wonderful was the dispensation of your mercy! Surely
the girl was thinking in her heart, 'This man is very like my
uncle in appearance'. But You alone, O God, lover of men,
from whom is all wisdom, guided matters lest she be over-

come with shame and run away. Yet this happened so that there might be a beginning with tears, so that the impossible might indeed come to pass and she might leave that place. Then the holy man offered the brothel-keeper the money he had brought and said to her, 'My friend, I want you to make us a very good meal, so that I may have this girl now; I have come a very long way out of love for her.' How true that was, according to God, a true spiritual word; what discretion was working towards salvation! Forty years of abstinence when he tasted nothing but bread, and now without hesitation he chewed meat to save a soul from hell! The choir of holy angels rejoiced and was amazed at his discretion, for without hesitation he ate and drank in order that he might draw a soul out of the mire! Wisdom of wisdom, understanding of understanding, discretion of discretion, come and let us wonder at his inexperience, at this alteration, how this man, wise, discreet and prudent, seemed a fool and indiscreet so that he might snatch from the mouth of the lion the soul it had eaten and set free from the darkness and bonds of sin the soul that had been taken and bound!

Cap. VIII. When they had eaten, the girl drew Abraham to the bed to lie down and took him towards the inner chamber, and he said, 'Let us go in.' When he got inside, he saw the bed set on a platform and he seated himself on it, as if eagerly. (What shall I say of you, athlete of Christ? Shall I speak of continence or incontinence, wisdom or foolishness, discretion or indiscretion? After forty years of conversion, you lie down on a prostitute's bed, and wait for her to come to you! All this you did for the praise and glory of Christ, undertaking the long journey to that house, eating flesh, drinking wine, entering a brothel, in order to save that lost soul. Now I must add salt to the words I use next, for this is the climax.)

Cap. IX. When he had seated himself on the bed, Maria said to him, 'Come, sir, let me unfasten your trousers for you'. And he said, 'First close the door carefully and lock it'. The girl wanted to unfasten him first but he would not let her. When she had locked the door, she came towards him and the old man said to her, 'Mistress Maria, come close to me.' And when she had come close he held her firmly with one hand, as if about to kiss her, but snatching the hat from

his head, in a voice breaking with tears, he said to her. 'Don't
you know me, Maria my child? Dear heart, am I not he who
took care of you? What happened, my dear? Who hurt you,
my daughter? What had become of the dress of angels that
you used to wear? What has become of your virginity, your
tears, your vigils, all your prayers? From what a height you
have fallen, my child, into such a pit as this! Why, when you
sinned, did you not tell me? Why could you not come and
speak of it with me? For of course I would have done penance
for you, I and our dearest Ephraim. Why did you not do that?
Why instead did you hurt me, and give me this unbearable
weight of grief? For who is without sin, save God alone?'
While he saying this and much besides, Maria sat like a stone
between his hands, overcome both by shame and fear. In
tears, the old man said to her, 'Why do you not speak to me,
my heart? Have I not come to take you home, my child? On
me be your sin, my daughter, and on the day of judgement I
will render an account of it for you to the Lord; it is I who will
be responsible for this to God.' And so until the middle of the
night Abraham consoled Maria with words of this kind, and
covered her with tears. After a while she plucked up courage
and, weeping, she said to him, 'I could not come to you; I was
so very much ashamed. How can I pray again to God when I
am defiled with sin which is as filthy as this?' The holy man
said to her, 'Upon me be your sin, Maria, and let God lay it to
my account. Only listen to me and come, let us go back
where we belong. See, our dearest Ephraim is grieving so
much for you and he is praying all the time for you to the
Lord. My dear, do not draw back from the mercy of God. To
you, your sins seem like mountains, but God has spread his
mercy over all that He has made. So we once read together
how an unclean woman came to the Lord and he did not send
her away but cleansed her, and she washed his feet with her
tears and wiped them with the hairs of her head. If sparks
could set fire to the ocean, then indeed your sins could defile
the purity of God! It is not new to fall, my daughter; what is
wrong is to lie down when you have fallen. Remember where
you stood before you fell. The Devil once mocked you, but
now he will know that you can rise more strong than ever
before. I beg you, take pity on my old age and do not make

me grieve any more. Get up and come with me to our cell. Do not be afraid; sin is only part of being human; it happened to you very quickly and now by the help of God you are coming out of it even more quickly, for he does not will the death of sinners, but rather that they may live.' Then she said to him, 'If you know of any penance I can do which God will receive from me, command me and lo, I will do it. Go first, and I will follow and I will kiss your footprints as I go. For you have so grieved for me that you came down even into this pit of filth in order to bring me out.' So she laid her head on his feet and wept away the rest of the night saying, 'What can I give to You, O Lord, to repay all that you have done for me?'

Cap. X. When morning came, blessed Abraham said to her, 'Get up, my daughter, and let us go home.' She said to him, 'I have this small amount of gold and these clothes, what do you want me to do with them?' And Abraham said, 'Leave it all here, Maria, for it came from evil'. So they got up and went out. He placed her on the horse and he went first leading it, like a shepherd with the lost sheep he had found, bearing it home upon his shoulders with joy. So with a glad heart Abraham made the journey home with his niece. When they arrived, he put her into the inner cell, and he himself stayed in the outside one. So she put on the hair shirt and in humility of soul and body she wore out her eyes with weeping, with vigils, with the most strict asceticism, praying constantly to the Lord in modesty and stillness, lamenting her sins in firm hope of forgiveness. She prayed so movingly that no one who heard her lamentation could refrain from weeping. Who would not give thanks for her to God? For her repentance was greater than all measure of grief. While she prayed to the Lord to forgive what she had done, she asked God also for a sign that this was accomplished. The most merciful God, who does not will that anyone should perish but that all should repent, having seen such repentance rewarded her prayers after three years by giving her the gift of healing. Crowds of people came to her daily and she would heal them all by her prayers for their salvation.

Cap. XI. So the blessed Abraham lived another ten years and he saw this great repentance and he glorified God. In the seventieth year of his age he slept in peace. For fifty years he had lived as a hermit with great endurance, humility of heart and love unfeigned.

Cap. XII. He did not take any notice of rank but was the same to the least as to the greatest, loving all, despising no one; he never changed his rule of abstinence nor did he let himself take it easy but lived as if he would die each day. This was the way of life of the most blessed Abraham and this was his way of struggle and conversion. He so withstood the bitter struggle against the Devil that he never retreated, nor did he relax his guard against the demons. Nor did he fear anyone, but the greatest and most wonderful fight he ever undertook was for the most blessed Maria; with spiritual wisdom and with all the ways of foolishness, he drew her back from hell. For what a wonder it was, when the serpent that entered his cell that night was indeed trodden under his feet and he snatched its prey from its grasp.

Cap. XIII. All this I have written for the consolation and help of all who want to undertake the monastic life, in piety and to advance quickly in it. I write also to the praise and glory of God whose overflowing grace is granted to us all. In fact, I wrote about most of the deeds of Abraham in a previous volume. At the moment of his death, almost all the city was gathered together and each one approached his dead body with reverence and took a piece of his clothing; and if anyone was sick, and these clothes touched them, they were healed without any delay.

Cap. XIV. Now Maria lived for another five years and continued her ascetic life, persevering day and night in weeping and tears, praying so much to the Lord that whoever came to that place and heard her, was at once moved and wept with her. At the hour when she fell asleep and was taken from this life, all who saw her glorified God because of the glory of her face.

Cap. XV. Alas as for me, for those two have fallen asleep and gone their way to the Lord in whom they believed! Their minds were never occupied with worldly business but only with the love of God. And I, unprepared and unfit, remain here, and lo, winter has overtaken me and the winds of infinity find me naked and poor and without a covering of good deeds. I sit here, and I wonder at myself, beloved, how I sin daily and daily mean to repent; each hour I try to build and each hour it all falls apart. Each evening, I say to myself, tomorrow I will repent and when next day dawns I pass the time away in pride; then at evening I say to myself, I will keep vigil tonight and I will pray to the Lord with tears so that he will have mercy on my sins, but when night comes, I fall asleep. Lo, those two who were with me have used well the talent of the daytime that was given them and have gone on to their reward and are set over ten cities; I, left behind, have hidden the talent of my time in the earth, and the Lord is about to reckon with me. So my heart quakes for my neglect of time and I have no excuse to offer.

Cap. XVI. Have mercy on me, God, alone without sin, and save me, for you alone are kind and merciful. For besides you and the only-begotten Son who became man for us, and the Holy Spirit who sanctifies all things, I know of no other nor do I believe in any other. Now remember me, Lover of men, and lead me out of the prison of my sins, for it was you who first willed me to enter the world and now you stand ready to bring me out of it. Remember me, for I have no protection, and save me, a sinner; and let those who were to me in this world a help, a refuge, and a glory, keep me under their wings from the day of terror and fear. You who see the heart, you know how greatly I have tried to avoid depravity and sin, vanity and especially heresy, by your grace which illuminates my soul. I pray you, holy Lord, save me in your kingdom, and deign to bless me, together with those who were so good in your sight, for to you alone belong glory and adoration and wonder, Father, Son and Holy Spirit, AMEN.

Conclusion

Mutual forgiveness of each vice
Opens the gates of paradise.[1]

These stories were told among the monks of the ancient
world and finally written down; they were translated into
Latin, and later into the various vernacular languages, and
continued to circulate freely during the Middle Ages in the
world of Western Latin Christianity. And they were as popular here as in the very different world which had produced
them. Mary, Pelagia, Thaïs and Maria all found a place in
monastic literature in the West, while the eleventh century
saw the cult of Mary Magdalene reach unparalleled heights of
popularity. It remains to ask, first, what is the essential message of these stories in their original context, and secondly, to
see if there is any appreciable difference in the way these
stories were presented in their new context.

From the fourth century onwards, these stories were told
and retold and shaped for the use of the monks. It is exactly
the monastic choice of chastity lived out as celibacy for life
that formed these stories. Their popularity among monks is
neither a sign of unhealthy repression leading to sexual fantasy and a prurient desire for stories about forbidden fruit,
nor are they in any way a part of the rejection of sexuality
which at times marks the writings of the early Church, particularly in the gnostic tradition. On the contrary, these
stories are about two facts of primary importance for monks:
the first is the clear recognition of the reality and force of
sexual desire in human experience; the second is the equally
clear realisation that such desire has a true and central role in
human life as desire for God, whether it is lived out in the
sacrament of marriage or in the sacrament of the monastic

102

life. Both are equally an image of the union between Christ and his Church. In these stories, the harlots present both themes dramatically, both the bondage of human desire and the fire of love that it can become. The monk tempted to sexual sin would find hope in these stories, the proud, self-assured monk would find all his assumptions challenged and changed. The idea that a monk can 'keep' a virginity of body by his own prudent behaviour is here shown to be facile. 'Virginity', they say in this tradition, 'is restored by tears', and these stories show that in fact it is also created by tears. The only virginity for the monk is Christ. All are sinners, alienated from God, no one having virginity either by nature or by works. There is no clear glass held up to reflect the true likeness of God except Christ. In the baptism of water which is renewed by the tears of repentance, the monk receives Christ as virginity. It is a free gift, as much for the good monks Zossima, Nonnus, Paphnutius and Abraham as for the harlots. The good monk who relies on his own virtue, in however small a degree, falls into despair, which is the real sin of mankind. A story from a Coptic collection of *apophthegmata* illustrates this theme very clearly:

> A brother fell into sin and took himself to Abba Macarius, weeping and saying, 'Pray for me, father, for I have fallen into sodomy; you already know I have fallen in this way.' Abba Macarius said, 'Take courage, my son, and lay hold of Him who has no time, no beginning, continuing for all eternity which has no end; He is the help of those who have no help save Him alone, His is the name sweet to each mouth, the only sweetness, the perfection of life, who has uncounted treasures of mercy, Our Lord Jesus Christ, our true God. May He be your strength and your help, may He pardon you. My son, I tell you this, if a virgin falls into sin and does not pretend about it, I tell you that because of her appearance of shame and the injuries done to her because of it, which she accepts with joy, Christ rejoices over His own as over a virgin. So it is for you also, my son, when you made known your shame, as it says in Holy Scripture, "Confess your sins one to another and pray for each other that you may be forgiven and you will be saved" (James 5.16) for as Peter said to the Lord, "how many

times should I forgive my brother, even unto seven
times?,'' then the good God said to him. ''I do not say
unto you seven times, but unto seventy times seven''
(Matt. 18.21–22).[2]

What concerned the monks of the early Church was only
one question: 'how can I be saved?' The literary tradition
from that world shows them discovering the meaning of the
'I' in that question by a genuine awareness of the force of
passion within themselves. Only when they had become
aware of the force of this disintegration within themselves
could they receive the gift of salvation which is Christ. In the
later circulation of the harlot stories in the West, this theme,
fundamental to Christianity, was still the main reason for
their popularity. When Hrotswitha, for instance, wanted to
illustrate this theme of the power of chastity, she chose the
stories of Thaïs and Maria for two of her plays. When Humbert of Romans chose examples for his preachers about repentance, he used Mary Magdalene, Mary of Egypt. Thaïs and
Pelagia.

There are, however, other kinds of interest shown in these
stories, in addition to this deeply theological and monastic
theme in the West in the eleventh century and after. In the
eleventh century, the trade of prostitution came under the
microscope of those newly concerned with defining christian
morality.[3] In the early days of the Church, prostitutes in the
cities of the ancient world were condemned for two reasons:
first, they were identified with actors, dancers, jugglers and
musicians, who gave public pleasure by the use of the body
for a fee;[4] and secondly, prostitutes were associated with
pagan rites and orgies, where their bodies incited others to
sin. John Chrysostom made this point when he was advocating the use of the psalms in private homes:

> Let us join psalmody to prayer so that our homes may be
> sanctified as our souls are by the blessings of heaven.
> Those who invite to their feasts comedians, dancers,
> women of evil life, call there at the same time the devil
> and all his cohorts and make their homes a theatre of war
> and innumerable dissensions (for it is there that are born
> jealousies, fornications, adulteries and a crowd of other

sins). So, on the other hand, he who invites the prophet-king (David) with his sacred harp calls at the same time Jesus Christ into the heart of his home.[5]

A prostitute was therefore excluded from receiving the sacraments[6] and this continued into the Middle Ages; her association with pagan rites naturally was of less interest as paganism receded from public notice. In the eleventh century, however, prostitution and its morality came into the general discussion about canon law on conduct. The new questions turned on the matter of the earnings of prostitutes. First, it was asked if money acquired by immoral acts could be rightfully retained by the recipient. The answer to this was 'yes': a prostitute acts immorally in what she does, but she does not receive money immorally because she is a prostitute.[7] The second question was, could a prostitute offer alms from her earnings? The answer was again, yes; with discretion alms might be given out of the earnings of a prostitute, but secretly to avoid scandal. This was given point when Maurice of Sully, bishop of Paris, was offered stained glass and chalices by prostitutes for the church of Notre Dame.[8] Stephen Langton thought he was free to accept such gifts but without making it known. The matter of alms from a prostitute's earnings had been a point of contention in the deserts of Egypt also; the solution reached by the harlots in the stories considered here was that at their conversion they should simply withdraw from their earnings and not try to do good with them in any way. One story, however, suggests a different attitude from at least one of the desert fathers:

> Abba Timothy the priest said to abba Poemen: 'There is a woman who commits fornication in Egypt and she gives her wages away in alms.' Abba Poemen said, 'She will not go on committing fornication, for the fruit of faith is appearing in her.' Now it happened that the mother of the priest Timothy came to see him, and he asked her, 'Is that woman still living in fornication?' She replied, 'Yes, she has increased the number of her lovers, but also the amount of her alms.' Abba Timothy told Abba Poemen. The latter said, 'She will not go on committing fornication.' Abba Timothy's mother came again and said to him, 'You know that sinner? She

wanted to come with me so that you might pray over
her'. When he heard this, he told Abba Poemen, and he
said to him, 'Go and meet her.' When the woman saw
him and heard the word of God, she was filled with compunction and said to him weeping, 'From today forward
I will cling to God and I resolve not to commit fornication any more'. She entered a monastery at once and was
pleasing to God.[9]

Abba Poemen was not interested in the morality of the use
of the money earned by the prostitute, but in her conversion.
This patient attitude of waiting for a true conversion of heart
to take place was not the way expressed in the rules of the
Church. Prostitutes came automatically under the ban of
excommunication, though Thomas Cobham thought they
should at least be allowed to enter the church and offer candles
on Sunday evenings with the other women; they could even,
he suggested, stay at the eucharist until the kiss of peace. But
there were harsher approaches: in 1263 Robert of Cousan had
prostitutes expelled from Paris and segregated like the
lepers.[10]

The concern which was paramount in the desert for the
conversion of prostitutes does not seem to have been promi-
nent in the West until the eleventh and twelfth centuries.
Then there grew up among monastic reformers and preachers
a new interest in the redemption of prostitutes. A possible
way out of such a life should, it was thought, be provided.
Innocent III, for instance, offered indulgences to those who
married reformed prostitutes.[11] Fulk of Neuilly, himself at
first a man of immoral life, after his conversion founded the
Cistercian convent of S. Antoine outside Paris for repentant
women of the streets.[12] The students of Paris contributed 250
pounds and the burgesses one thousand pounds to provide
dowries for prostitutes who wanted to leave their way of life
and marry.[13] At Fontevrault, Robert of Arbrissel and the
Abbess Petronilla created three monastic houses within one
complex: there was a house for the sick under the patronage
of St Benedict, one for lepers under the care of St Lazarus and
one for repentant prostitutes under the protection of St Mary
Magdalene. Robert of Arbrissel was himself particularly associated with the conversion of prostitutes.[14] It was said that

his preaching touched many of them and that they followed him; rumours even suggested that at night he would test his chastity by lying down to sleep among them.[15] Another more probable story was told about a visit he paid to a brothel on a cold winter's evening:

> He sat warming his feet surrounded by prostitutes. He preached to them the word of life and promised them the mercy of Christ. One of the prostitutes who was the leader among them said to him, 'Why are you speaking to us like this? It is twenty five years since I came into this house to do evil, and never has anyone come to speak to us about God or the mercy that would help us; now at last you have come, and I know it is true.'[16]

It seems quite possible that Robert, like other twelfth century preachers, found a ready audience among prostitutes for two reasons: first, the rise of the new devotion to the Passion of Christ and his sufferings on the cross[17] made much of Mary Magdalene at the foot of the cross, which gave those who were by definition 'sinful women' an obvious patron saint and helper. Secondly, there may well have been far more women described under this heading who were not 'prostitutes' by choice but simply the abandoned wives of those clergy who chose to follow the requirements of the Gregorian Reform for clerical celibacy; such women, used to hearing sermons, acquainted with christian doctrine and now without homes or means of support, would respond readily and with comprehension even to such complex preachers as Humbert and Fulk, and even more so to the warmth and simplicity of Robert.

Finally, there is another aspect of these stories which needs elucidation. These women sinned, repented and did not sin again; this is not the experience of the majority of christians. It is possible to identify with the harlots, in that all sin has the same root of alienation from God, from others and from ourselves; but it is more difficult to understand their apparent sinlessness thereafter. This is partly a matter of the literary form of the stories: they are about the free gift of the love of God to the soul, and at no point are they about the details of sinful behaviour; there is no more to be said about these women after the point is reached where they encounter the living grace of Christ as the central fact of their souls, and in each case no more is said; it is as if they were already dead. This does not, I think, mean that they were then in fact without awareness of sin in themselves; quite the contrary. Through the veil of discretion with which these silent years are protected, we glimpse the tears of Maria, the austerities of Pelagia, the burden of sins always before the eyes of Thaïs, the years of anguish of Mary of Egypt. Such details necessarily take up very little space in the stories which are about the journey towards the place of salvation, not a consideration of sins either before or after the encounter with Christ. Sin is the huge tragedy of mankind; it allures, fascinates, draws people into thinking about the sins and failures in themselves in a self-contemplation which can only increase despair; and where there is the least trace of despair there is the possibility of sin. These stories illustrate deliverance by Christ from this depair of the soul, ʹrom the risk of the tragedy of refusing life, of calling death life. Sin and life are inextricably mixed in mankind until death opens the way into a new dimension of life, and the stories of the harlots show people in whom this tension is most deeply experienced, and at last begins to be resolved when Christ is allowed to reach the ultimate block within them; that deep and cold conviction that they cannot love or be loved. At that point, these stories also show that the face of Christ, who alone has gone into the darkness of hell, is seen through others; with Mary of Egypt it is the face of the Mother of God; for Zossima it is the presence of Mary of Egypt herself; for Maria, the care of her uncle; for Thais, the presence of Paphnutius; and for Pelagia, the loving and mutual adoration between herself and the monk Nonnus. This illuminates the fact that Christ works his salvation through his new humanity, the people of God. The discovery of the freedom of Christ is always within the Kingdom, in community and relationship, both on earth and in heaven; it leads out of the isolation of sin and hell. The final image of the converted prostitute is not of an agonized, weeping penitent, but of one who has entered into the reality of love for God and therefore for all his creation:

Never has anything in this world been loved too much,
but many things have been loved in a false way; and all in
too short a measure . . . We should be all Life and Mettle
and Vigour and Love to everything; and that would
poise us. I dare confidently say that every person in the
whole world ought to be loved as much as this . . . but
God being beloved infinitely more will be infinitely
more our joy and our heart will be more with Him, so
that no man can be in any danger of loving others too
much who loveth God as he ought.[18]

NOTES FOR CONCLUSION

1. William Blake, *The Everlasting Gospel*.
2. *Les Sentences des Pères du Désert* (troisieme recueil), trad. by Lucien Regnault (Solesmes, 1976), Am. 187, 13, p. 184.
3. cf. John W. Baldwin and Milton R. Gutsch, *Masters, Princes and Merchants: the Social Views of Peter the Chanter and His Circle*, 2 vols. (Princeton, 1970), (hereinafter referred to as *Baldwin*).
4. *ibid.* vol. 1, cap. ix, pp. 198–204.
5. John Chrysostom, *Expositio in Psalmis* xli, PG 55, col. 158.
6. cf. N. M. Haring, 'Peter Cantor's Views on Ecclesiastical Excommunication, with practical consequences', *Medieval Studies*, X (1949), 101, 110.
7. *Baldwin*, vol. 1, cap. vi, p. 134.
8. *ibid.* p. 135.
9. *Sayings*, Timothy 1.
10. *Baldwin*, vol. 1, pp. 136–7.
11. Innocent 111, *Regesta*, PL 214, col. 102.
12. *Baldwin*, vol. 1, pp. 36–9.
13. *ibid.* vol. 1, p. 136.
14. cf. *L'impossible sainteté: la vie retrouvée de Robert d'Abrissel (v. 1045–1116), fondateur de Fontevraud,* Jacques Dalarun (Paris, 1985). Also Jacques Dalarun, *Robert d'Abrissel, fondateur de Fontevraud* (Paris, 1986).
15. *Lettre de Geoffroy de Vendôme*, PL 157, cols. 181–4. *Lettre de Marbode de Rennes*, PL 171, cols. 1480–92.
16. cf. 'L'Impossible sainteté' *op. cit.* pp. 121–2.
17. cf. R. W. Southern, *The Making of the Middle Ages* (London

1953), pp. 209–52, and B. Ward, *Prayers and Meditations of St Anselm* (introduction) (London, 1970 (1986)).

18. Thomas Traherne, *Centuries* (Oxford, 1963) II, 66 and 68, pp. 87–88.

Index

CISTERCIAN PUBLICATIONS INC.
Kalamazoo, Michigan

TITLES LISTING
THE CISTERCIAN FATHERS SERIES

Texts and Studies
in the
Monastic Tradition

* Temporarily out of print   *† Forthcoming*

THE CISTERCIAN STUDIES SERIES

Temporarily out of print   †Forthcoming

Eight Chapters on Perfection and Angel's Song
(Walter Hilton)

Creative Suffering (Iulia de Beausobre)

Bringing Forth Christ. Five Feasts of the Child
Jesus (St Bonaventure)

Gentleness in St John of the Cross

Distributed in North America only for Fairacres Press.

DISTRIBUTED BOOKS

St Benedict: Man with An Idea (Melbourne Studies)

The Spirit of Simplicity

Benedict's Disciples (David Hugh Farmer)

The Emperor's Monk: A Contemporary Life of
Benedict of Aniane

A Guide to Cistercian Scholarship (2nd ed.)

*North American customers may order
through booksellers or directly
from the publisher:*

Cistercian Publications
WMU Station
Kalamazoo, Michigan 49008
(616) 383-4985

*Cistercian Publications are available in
Britain, Europe and the Common-
wealth through A. R. Mowbray &
Co Ltd   St Thomas House   Oxford
OX1 1SJ.
For a sterling price list, please consult
Mowbray's General Catalogue.*

*Cistercian monks and nuns have been
living lives of prayer & praise, meditation &
manual labor since the twelfth century.
They are part of an unbroken tradition
which extends back to the fourth century
and which continues today in the Catholic
church, the Orthodox churches, the
Anglican communion, and, most recently,
in the Protestant churches.*

*Share their way of life and their search for
God by reading Cistercian Publications.*

*A complete catalogue of texts-in-
translation and studies on early,
medieval, and modern Christian
monasticism is available at no cost
from Cistercian Publications.*